YOURS
IS THE
CHURCH

How
Catholicism
Shapes
Our
World

MIKE AQUILINA

servant

AN IMPRINT OF
FRANCISCAN MEDIA
Cincinnati, Ohio

Scripture passages have been taken from the *Revised Standard Version*, Catholic edition. Copyright 1946, 1952, 1971 by the Division of Christian Education of the National Council of Churches of Christ in the USA. Used by permission. All rights reserved.
A quote is taken from the English translation of the *Catechism of the Catholic Church* for the United States of America (indicated as CCC), 2nd ed. Copyright 1997 by United States Catholic Conference—Libreria Editrice Vaticana.

Cover design by Candle Light Studios
Cover images © Shutterstock
Book design by Mark Sullivan

LIBRARY OF CONGRESS CATALOGING-IN-PUBLICATION DATA
Aquilina, Mike.
Yours is the church : how Catholicism shapes our world / Mike Aquilina.
p. cm.
Includes bibliographical references.
ISBN 978-1-61636-434-2 (alk. paper)
1. Catholic Church—Influence. 2. Christianity and culture. I. Title.
BX1795.C85A45 2012
282.09—dc23
2012028916

Published by Servant,
an imprint of Franciscan Media
28 W. Liberty St.
Cincinnati, OH 45202
www.FranciscanMedia.org

CONTENTS

Dedicated to the memory of
Father Ronald Lawler, Capuchin

INTRODUCTION

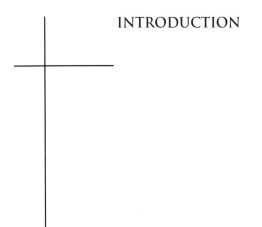

What has the Church ever done for humanity?

If you listen to popular culture today, you might get the impression that the Church is the universal enemy. The Church stands in the way of progress. It exploits the poor. It oppresses women and children. It condemns everything that's good in our culture. And above all, it stands opposed to science and reason.

You've heard it all so often that, even if you're Catholic, you might half-believe it. But it's all wrong, and this book is going to show you why.

There are lots of books about great Catholics who have also been scientists, musicians, artists, or leaders—people who have done some good in the world, even though they're Catholic. This book isn't like that. This book makes a much bigger and more startling claim: Everything about our modern world we think is good is there because of the Church.

The only reason we care about the poor is because Christianity has won. The only reason the rights of women and children are important is because the Church has made them important. The only reason we have science is because the Church taught us how to think.

This book is full of unbelievable statements like that. My hope is that, by the end of the book, you'll believe them all.

Yours is the Church that built up the best in modern culture. And yours is the Church that has constantly defended the best against the horrors that rise against it. It's an exciting story, roaming up and down through two thousand years of history. And perhaps the best place to begin is with the end of civilization.

CHAPTER ONE

Yours Is the Church That Saved Civilization

When we think of the beginning of modern civilization, we think of the Renaissance—that glorious rebirth when classical learning was rediscovered, when the arts took wing and soared to new heights. But where did all that classical learning come from? Where had it been hiding for a thousand years?

That's a very interesting story.

Decline and Fall

Classical civilization reached its peak of power, organization, and prosperity in the Roman Empire. And the Roman Empire reached its peak in the 100s. After that it was all downhill.

By the middle 200s the empire was in a sorry state. One emperor after another was assassinated; in the later 200s the average reign of an emperor was two years—a bit depressing when you consider that emperors held their positions for life. Rival claimants to the imperial throne amassed huge armies, warred against each other, and made wastelands of their battlefields. What had been a world of peace and prosperity surrounding the Mediterranean Sea was repeatedly divided into hostile subempires. Commerce dwindled;

1

the economy spiraled into depression. Devastating plagues added to the misery.

Finally, at the end of the 200s, Diocletian gained control of the whole empire and tried to put it back together. He imagined a system in which two main emperors would rule, one in the east and one in the west. Each of the emperors would bear the title "Augustus," and each Augustus would adopt a younger colleague, a "Caesar," who would share his rule and ultimately become Augustus when the previous one retired. Thus the empire would be assured of stable, continuous rule for centuries to come.

Of course, it all fell apart as soon as Diocletian retired. Instead of an orderly succession, there was a free-for-all. Soon there were six emperors running around, all claiming to be Augustus, all amassing armies and pummeling their rivals whenever they got the chance. The chaos and carnage went on until the year 312, when one of the contenders managed to win Rome and put down all opposition. His name was Constantine, and we remember him even more for one other fact of his life: Just before the great victory that finally brought peace to the empire, he declared himself a Christian.

The empire that Constantine took over was a wreck of a civilization. The population had dwindled; vast territories were left almost empty by endless wars. Worse than that, the internal weakness of the empire had encouraged hungry hordes of "barbarians" (meaning pretty much anybody who wasn't Roman) to make pillaging raids that would turn into conquests and resettlements.

The arts had suffered as much as the rest of civilization. For a hundred years, literature had been going through the motions. An author won praise by imitating the great models of the past, no matter how irrelevant they were to his present subject. Today, no one reads classical literature from the 200s, either in Greek or in Latin; most of it is intolerably dull. The rest of the arts were in no better shape.

You can see the decline of the arts in the Arch of Constantine, which still stands in Rome today. It was given to the city by the senate to commemorate Constantine's great victory, which saved Rome from a hated tyrant (or at least that's how the imperial spin doctors told the story). It's a typical Roman triumphal arch, but if you look more closely at its many sculptures, you can see that they aren't all original. Many of them are high-quality works that were looted from earlier monuments—as if there weren't any artists left who could do the job right.

Constantine's victory brought stability, and the stability brought something of a revival of Roman civilization. But it was a changed civilization. Now Christianity was the dominant religion; all the great thinkers and writers of the era were Christian. Paganism lingered for a long time in conservative areas—notably among the upper classes in the city of Rome. But there are no great pagan writers of the 300s and 400s. The great writers were St. Augustine, St. Jerome, St. John Chrysostom, and a dozen others who made up a Christian literary culture as glorious as the golden age of pagan literature.

In spite of the revival of Roman fortunes, the damage of the long period of anarchy could not be completely undone. Invaders pressed harder and harder on the empire. When a long war with the Persians required moving most of the legions out of the empire's western half to fight in the east, Teutonic tribes took advantage of the weakened defenses to overrun the western provinces. In

410, invading Goths actually sacked the city of Rome. The empire never recovered from the blow.

The End of Civilization

The 400s were a time of disasters for Rome and the western half of the empire. But the disasters were not bad enough to wipe out Roman civilization. Even what we call the "fall of Rome" in 476 was a strikingly anticlimactic affair.

The last emperor of the Western Empire, Romulus Augustulus, was sent into a dignified retirement with a pension. For all anybody knows, he may have lived a long and uneventful life after that. Odoacer, probably a Germanic chief, became king of Italy, but he ruled in the name of Zeno, head of the Eastern Empire. The rest of the government remained the same; the only change was at the top of the organizational chart.

A few years later Zeno grew tired of Odoacer and sent the Gothic chief Theodoric to replace him. Of course, Odoacer didn't give up without a fight, but Theodoric won. Almost immediately he set about restoring the city of Rome to some shadow of its former splendor.

In fact, Rome came to be in much better shape under Theodoric than it had been in the last few decades of the Western Empire. You can still see many marks of Theodoric's ambitious building program throughout the city. Theodoric also filled his court with the greatest intellects of the age. It looked as though the end of imperial rule had been if anything a revival of Roman civilization rather than a catastrophe.

In the late 400s, in spite of the disintegration of the Western Empire into various barbarian kingdoms, there was once again a lively appreciation of literature, even if it wasn't the sort of literature we think is worth reading today. Books were a common commodity, and every town had its booksellers. St. Sidonius Apollinaris, a Gallic gentleman of leisure who became a bishop (but never lost his taste for the good life), describes the pleasures of two aristocratic country houses near Nimes:

> From the first moment we were hurried from one plea-
> sure to another. Hardly had we entered the vestibule of
> either house when we saw two opposed pairs of partners
> in the ball-game repeating each other's movements as they
> turned in wheeling circles; in another place one heard
> the rattle of dice boxes and the shouts of the contending
> players; in yet another, were books in abundance ready
> to your hand; you might have imagined yourself among
> the shelves of some grammarian, or the tiers of the
> Athenaeum, or a bookseller's towering cases.[1]

Clearly this was still a literate civilization. In fact, the usual complaint about Sidonius and his contemporaries is that their writing is too civilized and bookish—too artificial, that is, relying on complex rhetorical technique rather than substance.

The decline of civilization was breathtakingly fast when it did come. Sidonius died in 489. Almost a century later, St. Gregory of Tours, another bishop in Gaul, undertook a history of the Franks, and this is how he began it:

> With liberal culture on the wane, or rather perishing, in
> the Gallic cities, there were many deeds being done both
> good and evil: the heathen were raging fiercely; kings were
> growing more cruel; the church, attacked by heretics, was
> defended by Catholics; while the Christian faith was in

general devoutly cherished, among some it was growing cold; the churches also were enriched by the faithful or plundered by traitors.

And no grammarian skilled in the dialectic art could be found to describe these matters either in prose or verse; and many were lamenting and saying, "Woe to our day, since the pursuit of letters has perished from among us and no one can be found among the people who can set forth the deeds of the present on the written page."

Hearing continually these complaints and others like them I [have undertaken] to commemorate the past, [in] order that it may come to the knowledge of the future; and although my speech is rude, I have been unable to be silent as to the struggles between the wicked and the upright; and I have been especially encouraged because, to my surprise, it has often been said by men of our day, that few understand the learned words of the rhetorician but many the rude language of the common people.[2]

Sidonius would have considered Gregory's Latin appallingly illiterate (in fact, etymologists study it as an example of how Latin was evolving into the Romance languages of today). But Gregory, "rude" though his Latin might have been, was the only bishop in Gaul literate enough to put pen to paper and write a book. "The pursuit of letters," which was one of the chief amusements of the upper classes in Sidonius's time, "has perished from among us." In one century the society went from mass-market publishing to illiterate bishops.

This decline was so steep that it would have been clearly observable over one human lifetime. And there was one man who lived at just the right time and in just the right place to observe the collapse and to do something about it.

Cassiodorus

Cassiodorus Senator (*Senator* was his name, not his title) was in the thick of every catastrophe that overwhelmed Italy in the 500s. The space that separates Sidonius from Gregory mirrors the time of Cassiodorus's life (he lived to be about a hundred years old) from roughly 485 to 585. He was a high official in Theodoric's court at Rome at a time when Theodoric was getting increasingly cranky and suspicious.

Theodoric was all too aware of what had happened to Odoacer, and he never trusted Constantinople. In his old age he began to see conspiracies everywhere, and some of his pet intellectuals fell victim to his paranoia. But perhaps he wasn't so paranoid. The Roman aristocracy was always privately contemptuous of the barbarian king, and what made it worse was that Theodoric was an Arian heretic rather than an orthodox Catholic. If it came down to a question of loyalty to Theodoric or to Constantinople, it was probably no injustice to the Roman upper classes to say that many of them would have chosen Constantinople.

After the death of Theodoric, dynastic squabbles weakened the Gothic kingship and gave Constantinople the opportunity it had probably been waiting for. When Justinian the Great came to the throne in 527, he brought a dream of taking back the whole Roman Empire from the barbarians who had taken big chunks of it. With the military genius Belisarius leading his armies, he very nearly succeeded. For a short time the Roman Empire once again surrounded the Mediterranean Sea, and the map of Justinian's territory looks something like the map of the empire in the time of Augustus.

At first, the Roman upper classes welcomed Justinian's reconquest: Justinian was a Latin-speaking Roman who would free them from the domination of Teutonic barbarians. (In fact, he would be the last native Latin speaker to hold the title of Roman emperor.) It seemed a restoration of the glorious Roman Empire. But if the old Roman senatorial class expected to come back into power, they were quite mistaken. Justinian sent his own Greek governors to administer his new possessions, completely ignoring the Roman aristocracy. The Greeks turned out to be as domineering as the Goths had been.

During much of this time, Cassiodorus was in Constantinople, studying and absorbing the culture of the greatest city in the Mediterranean world. He returned to Italy after its conquest was complete and found the country a wreck after two decades of war. Literate culture was rapidly declining, and the great country houses with their magnificent private libraries were abandoned ruins.

Then, just after Justinian died in 567, a new disaster came: The Lombards invaded from the north and set about knocking down whatever was left of Roman civilization. The governors sent from Constantinople, who were based not in Rome but in Ravenna, seemed powerless to stop the invaders and showed little interest in protecting anything but themselves.

Cassiodorus—by now a very old man—retired to his family estate in southern Italy, which was the part of the peninsula least affected by the catastrophes. There he founded a unique monastery called the Vivarium, where he began the project that made him one of the most important figures in the history of civilization. Gathering all the books he could find out of the wreckage that was Italy, Cassiodorus built a great library at the Vivarium. Then he made it one of the duties of the monks to copy those books so that they would be preserved and available for anyone who needed them.

It was a turning point in history. Other monasteries took up the idea, and soon copying books was one of the expected duties of a monk. Almost all we have of pagan antiquity comes to us because of the system of monastic copying that Cassiodorus invented. There would have been no Renaissance—no rebirth—if Cassiodorus had not seen the darkness falling and done what he could to keep the light burning.

Cassiodorus did not invent monasticism, and his monks were certainly not the first to devote themselves to study as well as prayer. But it was Cassiodorus who consciously made the monastery a fortress of learning. He insisted that his monks have a well-rounded education, both in the great works of Christian thought and in important secular books.

His idea continued to spread. At the very end of the world, in Ireland, monasteries also preserved literate culture. As conversions continued, the heathen Saxons and Angles in Britain turned into the pious and learned English. They in turn sent the great St. Boniface to enlighten their cousins in Germany.

All through the Dark Ages, such little sparks of light flashed from monastery to monastery across the darkened face of Europe. Whenever there was any light at all in the darkness, we know it was carried there by the Church. So it's not surprising that, when at last Charlemagne began his great attempt to revive culture and learning in the West, he brought in an English churchman to organize the effort.

Alcuin of York

Charlemagne (Old French for "Charles the Great") became King of the Franks in 768, and his territory grew to include most of modern France, Germany, and Italy. In 800 Pope Leo III, recognizing that the Roman emperors of the East had been useless to the West for about two hundred years, crowned Charlemagne emperor of the Romans.

Conquest was not Charlemagne's only ambition—not even his main ambition. He was genuinely interested in reviving Roman civilization, even if he wasn't very civilized himself. He learned his letters with great effort—in fact, he never quite mastered them—but he encouraged all his nobles to learn to read. There was doubtless much grumbling; reading was something done by effete clerics, not Frankish nobles. Imagine our Secretary of the Army decreeing that every drill sergeant must learn ballet, and you can get an idea of how Charlemagne's suggestion struck the average Frankish duke or count.

At court, Charlemagne surrounded himself with the greatest minds of the age. They were all churchmen, of course—there simply weren't any secular intellectuals left. To Alcuin of York, an English cleric widely considered the smartest man in Western Europe at the time, he entrusted the project of spreading literacy. He couldn't have made a better choice.

Alcuin set up a *scriptorium*—a writing factory—in Charlemagne's capital at Aachen, where he set monks to copying all the books he could get his hands on. All the great works of Latin antiquity went through Alcuin's book mill, and the manuscripts were distributed far and wide. When Alcuin became bishop of Tours, the copying continued there.

In spite of his all-out efforts, Alcuin couldn't turn Charlemagne's empire into a polite and literate society in one generation. The world wasn't ready for the Renaissance yet; there was a lot of work to be done first. Already, in the generation after Charlemagne died, the intellectuals he had so carefully nurtured could see the darkness falling again. When a monk named Walafrid wrote a preface to the life of Charlemagne he was copying, he was already looking back to the great king's reign as a golden age of intellectual accomplishment.

> ...Now, Charles was beyond all kings most eager in making search for wise men and in giving them such entertainment that they might pursue philosophy in all comfort. Whereby, with the help of God, he rendered his kingdom, which, when God committed it to him, was dark and almost wholly blind (if I may use such an expression), radiant with the blaze of fresh learning, hitherto unknown to our barbarism. But now once more men's interests are turning in an opposite direction, and the light of wisdom is less loved, and in most men is dying out.[3]

But it would not be quite so dark a darkness as before Charlemagne. Alcuin had done his job too well for that. In spite of a new wave of barbarians—the Vikings—more terrible than those who had brought down Rome, books still multiplied.

You don't have to look any further than this page to see the effect Alcuin had on European civilization. Look at the letters in front of you. The capital letters are the old Roman alphabet, but most of the marks on this page are the letters Alcuin left us.

In the darkness before Charlemagne, it had been almost a point of pride among the few literate clerks that their letters were both hard to make and hard to decipher. But if everyone was going to read, then there wasn't time for that nonsense. Alcuin's massive book-production program demanded a script that was not only easy to read but also quick to write. His copyists used a style we call "Carolingian minuscule." It is probably the only medieval script that the average reader of today would have no trouble interpreting.

The reason we use Alcuin's minuscule has to do with his other great accomplishment. He really did succeed in multiplying books to a prodigious extent. Over and over we find that the oldest surviving manuscript of a well-known classical work comes from the time of Charlemagne and is written in Carolingian minuscule. When Renaissance scholars read those manuscripts, they mistakenly dated them to the classical era, and they copied the tidy Carolingian minuscule thinking they were reviving the ancient Roman style of writing. Early printers in Italy and France made their types in the same Renaissance style, setting what became the pattern for printing throughout Western Europe.

Probably nine out of ten of the books Sidonius could have bought at his local bookseller had vanished by Alcuin's time. But very little of classical antiquity has been lost since then. Once again the Church saved civilization.

Alcuin could hardly have hoped to succeed as well as he did. His efforts brought classical civilization back from the brink of extinction. And even though the world wasn't quite ready for another great intellectual age, Alcuin gave future thinkers the materials they would build on for centuries. When that next great age of learning did come, it would owe everything to Alcuin and the monks who worked under him.

CHAPTER TWO

Yours Is the Church That Nurtured Modern Science

If you read popular histories or magazine articles, you might think that the story of modern science is one of brave thinkers fighting the Church for the right to find the truth. That is almost exactly backward. The story of modern science is one of brave thinkers who found their refuge from an often dark and hostile world in the one place where the lights were still on: the Church.

Astronomy? Nicholas Copernicus was an ordained canon who spent his whole career in the service of the Church.

Geology and paleontology? It was a Catholic bishop, Nicholas Steno, who laid the foundations on which both sciences were built.

Chemistry? St. Albert the Great, doctor of the Church, liberated chemistry from the superstitions of alchemy, and the greatest name in modern chemistry, Antoine Lavoisier, was a devout Catholic who died a martyr in the French Revolution.

Genetics? A monk, Gregor Mendel, figured out the fundamental principles of heredity.

Logic? St. Thomas Aquinas reached back to Aristotle to codify the reasoning that all modern science depends on.

When we trace the history of modern science, we find that it all has its roots in the Catholic Church. Wonderful things began to happen there in what we call the High Middle Ages.

A Gift From the Muslim World

Cassiodorus limited his recommended readings to Latin writers, because he took it for granted that most of his monks would be ignorant of Greek. There had been a time, a few centuries earlier, when every educated Roman knew Greek and when learned treatises were expected to be written in Greek, in the same way that modern botanists were expected to write their descriptions in Latin until the year 2012. But by Cassiodorus's time, the knowledge of Greek had almost disappeared, even among the educated classes in the West.

Cassiodorus himself, of course, was a fluent speaker of Greek, having lived two decades in Constantinople. But he recognized that it was useless to include Greek writers on his list of basic works for the education of Italian monks. Thus the revival of learning in Charlemagne's time was almost exclusively a revival of Latin learning. What Western Europeans knew of Aristotle and Plato came from Latin summaries and incidental references in Latin writers. Imagine that all our knowledge of Einstein came from a high school physics textbook, and you have a fair idea of what people in Western Europe knew about Aristotle.

But about two centuries after Charlemagne, some of the old Greek philosophy began to trickle into the West—and from an unexpected source. It didn't come from Constantinople, where the Greek classics were still widely available and well known. It came from Spain.

Most of Spain at that time was a Muslim caliphate, but the population was a wonderfully diverse mix of Muslims, Christians, and Jews, each group with its own lively traditions and schools of philosophy, and all trading ideas back and forth. One of the ideas the Muslim side had to trade was Aristotle. At just about the time of Charlemagne, a wave of Aristotelian scholarship had passed through the Muslim world. Muslim philosophers in the East picked up the knowledge of Aristotle from their Greek-speaking Christian neighbors and ran with it. The works of Aristotle, translated into Arabic, were everywhere in the Muslim world.

In 1085, the city of Toledo, until then the capital of the caliphate, was conquered by the Christian king of Aragon. Suddenly that enormous library of classical wisdom was in Christian hands. Christian and Jewish scholars translated both the works of Aristotle and the writings of some of the great Muslim philosophers into Latin, the common language of learning in the West. When these translations started filtering into the rest of Europe, bells rang and lights flashed in the minds of the greatest thinkers of the time.

Of course, it goes without saying that all those great thinkers were in the Church. There simply wasn't anywhere else where thinking was *done*.

Albert the Great

One of the greatest of these medieval thinkers to take up Aristotle was a German monk, and later bishop, named Albert. Today we know him as Albertus Magnus, or Albert the Great, because he could think rings around almost anyone else alive.

Albert was the greatest scientist of his age. That might not have been hard in a time when "science" wasn't very well developed, but Albert would have been one of the greatest scientists in any age. His comprehensive proof that the world was round pretty much settled the question for the medieval world. Not long after Albert, a book later translated by William Caxton as *The Mirror of the World*—common knowledge for every educated person—explained the shape of the earth with everyday comparisons:

> If it so happened that there were nothing upon the earth—neither water nor any other thing that hindered and troubled the way in whatsoever part a man would go—he might go round about the earth, were it man or beast, above and under, whichever part he liked, as a fly goes round about an apple.... And if he went forth always in front of him, he should go so far that he should come again to the place from whence he first departed.[1]

Three hundred years later, Christopher Columbus would use that common knowledge that Albert had pulled from Aristotle: If the world was round, then couldn't he get to the East by going west?

Albert also tried real experiments in chemistry at a time when alchemists still thought they could make gold out of lead. (Albert insisted that it wasn't possible and, of course, he was right.) In fact, many scientists would call him the father of the experimental method.

Albert was the great botanist of the Middle Ages and possibly the greatest botanist of all time until the modern era. He knew more about physics than anyone else of his time. He studied the habits of animals with a scientific eye. He understood anatomy better than anyone else.

All these things could actually be dangerous knowledge in the 1200s. Scientific experiments were hard to tell from magic in an age that was just waking up from a long night of ignorance. There are persistent stories (probably false) that Albert's friend Roger Bacon was imprisoned for sorcery because of his scientific experiments. Medieval legend even made Albert a magician.

Albert understood how to be right without being arrogant. He was, first of all, a great Christian. He also knew how to be polite and persuasive when he was presenting his ideas. And that was terribly important, because there would come a time when he would have to fight for them.

Thomas Aquinas

If there was one thinker of the 1200s who could outthink Albert, it was Thomas Aquinas. In fact, St. Thomas was Albert's most brilliant student.

Thomas was born in 1225 in the little Italian city of Aquino, where his parents were rich enough to have a castle of their own. They had plans for him, a younger son, to join a respectable monastic order, which in those days would have meant being able to keep most of the aristocratic comforts of home. But Thomas was drawn to the Dominicans, who were anything but respectable. Dominicans took their vows of poverty very seriously: They renounced all worldly possessions and lived like poor people.

The idea of their son's running off to join some crazy cult like that was terribly distressing to Thomas's respectable parents—so much so that, when Thomas did leave to join the Dominicans, his parents sent his brothers to waylay him on the road. They easily overpowered Thomas and dragged him back to the family castle, where he was kept a prisoner for two years. An old legend says that his brothers, trying to make Thomas see reason, sent a prostitute in to seduce him and give him a taste for the delights of the flesh. Thomas grabbed a flaming log from the fire and chased her out of the room with it. Eventually, seeing that her son would never give up, his mother deliberately looked the other way while he escaped.

The Dominicans, as it turned out, were not revolutionary just in their way of life; they were also in the thick of the heady intellectual awakening that was surging through Europe in the 1200s. The Dominicans sent Thomas to the University of Paris, where he met Albert, who recognized his amazing intellect. This was something most people didn't recognize, since Thomas preferred listening to talking.

Thomas soon began a career of incredible productivity. Volume after volume flowed from his pen—or rather his secretaries' pens, since he usually dictated his books. He wrote so much that legend said he could miraculously bilocate—that is, be in two different places at the same time. The truth was scarcely less marvelous. He sometimes kept four secretaries going at once, working on four different books. He would run over to one as a thought for a book occurred to him and then dash to another with a thought for another book.

Thomas's greatest work, the *Summa Theologica,* fills several thick volumes of small type. It's nothing less than a complete (well, *almost* complete) encyclopedia of Catholic doctrine, all worked out with the logic Thomas had learned from Aristotle. Thomas's unique and provocative method was to ask the big, important questions ("Is there a God?"), giving the very best possible arguments *against* Christian doctrine ("It would seem that there is no God, because..."). Then he would carefully demolish those arguments.

The Legacy of Thomas and Albert

It was not an easy thing to bring the works of Aristotle—a pagan philosopher who had sneaked into Christendom through the Muslim back door—back from the dead. There were plenty of suspicious conservatives who thought that moldy old pagan philosophers and their ideas should just be left to molder. All his life Thomas had to deal with doubters who couldn't understand how Aristotle could have anything useful to say to Christians.

There's an old story that says Thomas's works narrowly escaped the flames. After his death in middle age, the debate raged in Paris: Should the innovations of Thomas be condemned? The reactionaries were gaining the upper hand. It looked as if the whole progress of European thought might be stopped in its tracks.

Suddenly the great Albert, by now a very old man, appeared at the door. He had walked for miles in the cold of winter to defend the legacy of his star pupil. With dignity and eloquence he argued that faith and reason can never be opposed, because God is rational. The same God who created the world gave us our reason so that we could understand it. Albert's gift for persuasion carried the day, and science was saved.

It's such a great story that it's a shame we don't really know if it's true. But even if it's only a legend, it tells us a lot about what a turning point Thomas's and Albert's works were in the history of thought. These two men gave Europe the idea of a rational universe, on which all scientific progress depends. The people who told the story of Albert's defense understood what was at stake, that everything science has accomplished since the 1200s depends on the idea of a rational universe. That is the legacy of Thomas Aquinas, Albert the Great, and the other great thinkers of the Middle Ages.

Today we number Albert and Thomas among the doctors of the Church—the great teachers whose works have made an exceptional contribution to our understanding of Christian truth. In fact, when the cause for Thomas's canonization was being debated, the devil's advocate (whose job it was to present all the evidence against the candidate) objected that there were no miracles attributed to Thomas. But his supporters had an answer for that. "There are as many miracles," one of the cardinals replied, "as there are articles in the *Summa*." Fifty years after he died, Thomas Aquinas was declared a saint.

Now, why is it so important that Thomas and Albert won this argument? Because this victory is actually the basis of all science; it is the reason why rational science made such astonishing leaps forward in the West when it was "stillborn" (as physicist and historian Fr. Stanley Jaki put it) in every other culture. Many great discoveries were made in China, in India, in Mexico, and all around the world. But only in the Christian West did science become an unstoppable locomotive that made one astonishing discovery after another. And it all goes back to the core of what Thomas and Albert believed: that God is completely and purely rational.

If God were irrational, then we couldn't really know anything about his creation. He might do things for any whimsical reason. An irrational god might favor Trojans one day, Greeks the next. Even if we were to figure out one thing about the world, that wouldn't tell us about anything else. If something happened that we didn't understand, we might just as well say that the god was in one of his moods again.

But if God is rational, then human reason is one of the ways we know God. The world is put together in such a way that we can use reason to understand it. One discovery leads to another, because the world is built everywhere on the same fundamental principles. The knowledge that God is rational leads straight to the great discoveries of Copernicus and all the other names we remember from the history of science.

Copernicus

We remember Copernicus for his astronomy, but the breadth of his knowledge was astonishing. He devoted his life to study in Church institutions, from the local cathedral school when he was a boy to the Universities of Krakow and Bologna. He was a doctor of canon law and an expert medical doctor, and in the Church he held the position of canon of Warmia, in northeast Poland. He spoke Latin as easily as he spoke Polish and German, and he knew Greek as well, giving him access to the works of the great Greek philosophers in their own language. But astronomy was the thing he really loved.

In those days, the ancient Greek writer Ptolemy was the last word in astronomy. The Ptolemaic system was *geocentric:* it put the earth at the center, with the sun and all the planets revolving around it. It was very good at predicting the positions of the planets, but those predictions required complicated circles on circles.

Ptolemy had heard of another Greek philosopher who had proposed a *heliocentric* system: the sun at the center, with the earth going around it. Ptolemy knew that the geometry of such a system was much simpler. But it was just too absurd to imagine the solid earth we all stand on flying through space like that!

Copernicus, however, was intrigued by the simplicity of the heliocentric system. The more he thought about it, the more the obviousness of it appealed to him. Instead of complex circles on circles, and sometimes circles on circles on circles, the diagram of the "universe" (meaning then what we call the solar system today, the stars being more or less infinitely far away) was wonderfully simple and elegant. And the more he looked at the night sky, the more simple and elegant it seemed.

Copernicus wrote some notes about his theory, and even in that sketchy form they passed from one astronomer to another, lighting fires in their minds. Eventually the news reached Rome, where Pope Clement VII himself sat in on some lectures about the new heliocentric theory. One of the cardinals present wrote to Copernicus and begged him to send as much information about his theory as possible.

It is interesting to note that the Protestant rebellion was just beginning in Germany at this time, and the Protestants had also heard of Copernicus's work. They thought it was ridiculous. Philip Melanchthon, the Lutheran leader, thought that secular rulers ought to suppress such nonsense. But yours is the Church that actually asked Copernicus to publish his work.

It took Copernicus years to put it all together in a book, but finally, just before his death, the great work was published—with a dedication to the new pope, Paul III. A preface added by the publisher explains that the new theory is merely a way of simplifying our calculations—it doesn't mean that the earth *really* moves. No one knows exactly how Copernicus felt, although it's probable that he thought the earth really did move.

We do know that many of the astronomers who came after Copernicus were convinced by the simplicity of his system. If God really were rational, then this seemed to be the way he would create the universe. That faith in a rational universe was the legacy of Thomas and Albert.

The Trouble With Galileo

And so we come to the one thing everyone remembers about the Church and science—and it happens to be an occasion when the Church's leaders were on the wrong side.

Galileo Galilei was, by any standard, a brilliant man. He performed experiments that formed the basis for all our modern knowledge of astronomy. He built one of the first practical telescopes and found amazing things in the sky, including the moons of Jupiter. And his astronomical observations convinced him that the heliocentric model of the universe—the system of Copernicus—was more than just a mathematical theory. It was the way the world really worked.

Galileo's friends in the Church wanted him to present the Copernican system as a mathematical model, a way of simplifying our calculations in astronomy. Pope Urban VIII, a longtime friend of Galileo, actually urged him to publish a book on the subject. Urban was a believer in the geocentric system, but he knew there were good arguments on the other side. Write a book with the best arguments on both sides, he said. I'll give you my best arguments for the geocentric system, and you can put them in with your best arguments for the heliocentric system.

So Galileo wrote a book called *Dialogues Concerning the Two*

Chief World Systems, which was cast as a series of conversations among three men: Salviati, the advocate of the heliocentric system; Simplicio, the advocate of the geocentric system; and Sagredo, the impartial observer who has to judge between them. The book wasn't quite what the pope had in mind. If you know something about Italian, you can see the problem right away in the names of the characters: *Salviati* means "wise," and *Simplicio* means "simpleton." In the dialogues, Pope Urban's best arguments are put in the mouth of Simplicio, and the other two characters make a fool of him.

So much for having the pope on Galileo's side.

Galileo also started getting stubborn about his science. He was sure that the earth moved, but to prove it he made some scientific assertions that were demonstrably wrong—for example, that the earth's rotation was the cause of the tides. Some of the best minds in the world were ranged against Galileo: He couldn't slip that stuff past them. And because he was so stubborn about things they could prove were wrong, they weren't as willing to give him a fair shake on the rest of his theories.

In the end Galileo was brought before the Inquisition on suspicion of heresy, and he was forced to recant his assertion that the earth actually moved around the sun. An old legend says that, while he was signing the document, he mumbled to himself, "But it *does* move."

The "Galileo affair," as everybody calls it, certainly was a "tragic mutual incomprehension," as Pope John Paul II called it—one that might have been avoided with a little more patience on both sides.[2] Pope Urban might have been Galileo's staunchest ally, even when the two men disagreed on scientific questions, but Galileo chose to ridicule him in a very public way. Pope he may have been, but Urban was only human. Galileo had deliberately made a fool of him, and he was not feeling very indulgent anymore.

It's worth noting that, in spite of the personal insults, the Inquisition came down very lightly on Galileo. His confinement was at a beautiful villa, not in a dank prison. He continued his scientific work, and some of his most important contributions to science came after his trial.

But if Galileo was rude and tactless, the Inquisition was just plain wrong about the Copernican system, and we can't forget that. The stubbornness on both sides had far-reaching effects. Books that advocated the Copernican system—at least as a reality, rather than as merely a mathematical model—were officially banned for years afterward.

The human beings who have to administer Christ's Church do make mistakes. But the Church also corrects such mistakes. In 1741 the works of Galileo were issued in a new edition—with an imprimatur arranged by Pope Benedict XIV himself.

We've probably spent too much time on Galileo. His case was an anomaly in the history of a Church that, for centuries, had been not only friendly to science but in fact the only outlet for it. But the Galileo story has become such a pervasive myth in pop culture that we have to understand what really happened. It's true that the people who judged for the Church were wrong. They made a bad mistake. It's also true that the Church corrected that mistake because the evidence in favor of the heliocentric system was overwhelming.

One last thing to remember: There would have been—in fact, could have been—no Galileo if there had been no Thomas and

Albert. Galileo's discoveries in physics and astronomy are essential foundations for modern science. But the essential foundation of Galileo's discoveries is the idea of the rational universe, the idea that Thomas Aquinas stated so forcefully and Albert the Great defended so graciously.

Pascal and Steno

The best proof that the Galileo affair was an anomaly is the long list of amazing minds that have come out of the Catholic Church in the time since then. Think of Blaise Pascal, for example. By the age of sixteen, he had already made such brilliant discoveries in mathematics that René Descartes, the most famous mathematical mind in France, refused to believe that the work had come from a sixteen-year-old boy.

At nineteen, Pascal invented a mechanical computer to help his father (a tax collector) deal with the complicated non-decimal system of French money, and we can draw a line from that machine straight to the computer on your desk or the smartphone in your pocket. His experiments with fluids proved the existence of a vacuum—something that Descartes and nearly every other scientist in the world had agreed could not exist.

Yet in spite of his brilliant scientific mind—or perhaps we should say because of it—Pascal became more and more deeply religious, and he devoted the last years of his all-too-brief life to a search for higher truth. His *Pensées* or "Thoughts"—scattered notes for a book he never finished—are still making conversions today: An encounter with Pascal's brilliant mind is an unforgettable and life-changing experience.

As much as for any of his enormous contributions to science, we remember him for "Pascal's Wager," his simple but almost unanswerable argument for putting his faith in God. Assume that we can't prove by reason that God exists or that he doesn't. But we do have to bet on one or the other: Either God does exist or he doesn't. If we bet on God's existence, we stand to gain everything if we win, but we lose nothing if we lose. Therefore, the only reasonable choice is to bet that God exists.

Nicholas Steno is another great name in the history of science. He was born in 1638 to a respectable Lutheran family in Copenhagen, and he started his scientific career by questioning the received wisdom about certain facts of anatomy. He made discoveries in that science that still bear his name. He also made the whole science of paleontology possible by rejecting the almost universally accepted notion that fossils somehow grew in the earth. Steno demonstrated that they were actually the remains of ancient life.

Meanwhile, that same talent for questioning received wisdom led Steno to another startling discovery. While traveling in Italy, he happened to see a Corpus Christi procession. It started him wondering: Could it be that the Catholic Church was right after all? He approached the problem the same way he approached his science: by studying all the evidence, thinking hard, and not taking anything for granted. After much soul-searching, and though it cost him a very promising university career in Denmark, he entered the Catholic Church.

Steno continued his scientific work, laying the scientific foundations for geology. He also discovered Steno's Law of Constant Angles in crystallography, showing that the angles on the surface of a crystal are always the same in the same kind of crystal. This again is one of the founding laws of the science.

The sacrifice Steno made in giving up his career wasn't without its compensations. Even while he was publishing some of his most revolutionary scientific work, Steno immersed himself in theology. In 1675 he was ordained a priest, and five years later he was made a bishop, gaining a reputation for holiness as well as scientific brilliance. He was beatified by Pope John Paul II, so today we know him as Blessed Nicholas Steno.

Science Marches On

There aren't enough pages in this book to list the great scientists whose Catholic faith existed side by side with their scientific method in the search for truth. Think of Lavoisier, the founder of modern chemistry, for example—a man who was keenly interested in showing that the Catholic faith had a rational basis. He was also keenly interested in the plight of the poor. He worked hard for reform of the French government—only to die a martyr during the French Revolution for the crime of having had something to do with the former government.

Or think of Gregor Mendel, the Austrian monk who—working alone and unnoticed—discovered the principles of heredity that form the basis of the science of genetics. No one paid attention to him at the time, but after his death his articles were rediscovered, and today we refer to the basic properties of inheritance as "Mendelian."

Catholic thinkers have been at the forefront of some of the most surprising and challenging ideas of the last century. For example, the "big bang" theory—the idea that the whole universe originated in one primordial singularity—came from Monsignor Georges Lemaître, a Belgian priest and professor. His bold proposal at first shocked the top names in science, Einstein for one. But he won them over with his solid mathematical demonstrations. Today Monsignor Lemaître's work is the basis of all our modern astronomical theory.

Or take the digital computer, perhaps the biggest revolution in our way of life since the printing press. Pascal gave us the basis of computing, but the way digital computers work today has a lot to do with the work of John von Neumann. Von Neumann was baptized in the Catholic Church when he married a Catholic, and then he fell away from the Church when his marriage fell apart. But toward the end of his life, he turned back to the Church—perhaps finding a truth there beyond what mathematics and quantum mechanics could give him.

And what about the future? Will the Catholic Church still be the cradle of scientists, or have science and religion somehow drifted apart in our generation?

No one can tell who will make the next brilliant discovery or provide the next mind-bending theory of the cosmos that will organize all our knowledge into elegantly simple equations. But one thing we can see right now: In the United States, Catholic school students on average score consistently higher on standardized tests in mathematics and science than public school students do.[3] This gives us good reason to suspect that the next big thing in science may well come from someone who grew up in the Catholic Church.

CHAPTER THREE

Yours Is the Church of Charity

"The world before Christ came was a world without love."[1]

That's a stark way of putting it, but that was the conclusion of one famous nineteenth-century historian when he looked at pagan antiquity before the Christian revolution. It's not that mothers never loved their children, or husbands their wives. Natural human love is planted in us from the beginning of creation. And sympathy of one human being for another's misfortune is wired into our nature; thus beggars might survive on the coins passersby tossed to them.

But the idea of universal love was something new and, to pagan thinking, quite obviously wrong. People had to prove they were worth something; they didn't earn respect just by being human. A beggar was a failure. A slave was inferior by nature. The members of the aristocracy were better than other people—in fact, the Greek word *aristocracy* quite literally means "rule of the best."

Then came these Christians with their absurd idea "Blessed are the poor in spirit"! They took care of the poor—even the pagan poor. What were they up to?

Philanthropy and Charity

It wasn't that the pagan aristocracy never did anything public-spirited. On the contrary, wealthy Romans were big on philanthropy. They donated buildings and entertainments to the people of the city, because that was what one did to maintain one's social position. A public official had to be memorably lavish with his philanthropy if he expected to advance to a higher position. The more ambitious he was, the more lavish he would have to be. This was how the empire obtained its public works.

If you go to Rome today, you can still see the name of the donor written on the front of the Pantheon, the most famous ancient temple left in the city: Marcus Agrippa, spelled out in letters as tall as Marcus Agrippa himself.

In other words, Roman philanthropy was really a matter of drawing attention to the philanthropist. It was not a response to the needs of the poor; in fact, the more gaudy and useless the display, the more effective it was at producing the proper impression of lavish generosity.

On the other hand, there were the Christians. In the first three centuries of the Church, few of them had much money to speak of: A prominent aristocrat who turned Christian was liable to have his wealth confiscated. Lavish displays weren't their thing. In fact, their Teacher had told them, "When you give alms, do not let your left hand know what your right hand is doing, so that your alms may be in secret; and your Father who sees in secret will reward you" (Matthew 6:3–4).

Obviously, this was exactly the opposite of Roman philanthropy. Christian charity responds to someone's need without asking, "What's in it for me?" This is the kind of giving that Christ expects of us. "Give to every one who begs from you," he said, "and of him who takes away your goods do not ask them again" (Luke 6:30).

Writing in about AD 200, when Christians were still a persecuted minority, Tertullian tried to explain to suspicious and hostile pagans how Christians lived.

> That kind of treasury we have is not filled with any dishonorable sum, as the price of a purchased religion; every one puts a little to the public stock, commonly once a month, or when he pleases, and only upon condition that he is both willing and able; for there is no compulsion upon any: all here is a free-will offering, and all these collections are deposited in a common bank for charitable uses, not for the support of merry meetings, for drinking and gormandizing, but for feeding the poor and burying the dead, and providing for girls and boys who have neither parents nor provisions left to support them, for relieving old people worn out in the service of the saints, or those who have suffered by shipwreck, or are condemned to the mines, or islands, or prisons, only for the faith of Christ; these may be said to live upon their profession, for while they suffer for professing the name of Christ, they are fed with the collections of his Church.[2]

It's worth noting that Tertullian mentions all the things Christians do for the poor in the context of Christian worship.

The "collections" he describes were those taken up at Mass. To Christians, then as now, charity and worship are inseparable. That gives Christians a completely new way of seeing the relationship between rich and poor.

The First Shall Be Last

To pagan thought, wealth was at least no barrier to virtue. The ordinary citizen in the Roman Empire probably believed without thinking about it what the word *aristocracy* implied: that wealthy families really were better than the rest.

Christians, on the other hand, not only rejected wealth as a measure of worth but actually went to the opposite extreme. "It is easier for a camel to go through the eye of a needle," Jesus said, "than for a rich man to enter the kingdom of God" (Mark 10:25). We have good evidence that Christians took this saying seriously and sometimes even went a bit overboard. St. Clement of Alexandria, who lived only about a century after Christ, felt that he had to remind his flock not to treat the rich with open contempt:

> If you love truth and you love your brothers, you won't be rude and insolent toward the rich who are called. Nor will you flatter them for your own greedy reasons. Instead, take away their groundless despair with Scripture. Interpret the Lord's revelation rightly, showing why the Kingdom of Heaven is not completely out of their reach if they obey the commandments.[3]

Flattering the rich was natural enough, but who ever heard of the opposite—treating people with contempt because they were rich and successful? Yet that was the danger Christians had to be warned against—so completely had they absorbed Christ's saying, "But many that are first will be last, and the last first" (Mark 10:31).

The Misery They Faced

The charity of the Christians was all the more striking because the need for it was so great. Roman cities were filled with misery almost beyond our capacity to imagine. One saw it everywhere: the beggar covered with boils sitting on the corner, the man with one leg hobbling down the street, the mother wailing for her dead child. Disease was everywhere, and even in times of peace, catastrophe was common. Shabbily built apartment houses would fall in and kill all the residents. Murder and other crimes were rampant.

And every once in a while the plague would come to town, so that everyone could be miserable at once. The wealthy would flee to their country houses, hoping to stay one step ahead of the contagion. Leading the exodus would be the doctors, who knew the signs of an approaching epidemic as well as the fact that they couldn't do anything to stop it.

Pagan priests, too, would be among the first to go: They were wealthy and influential, and their job description didn't include hanging around a bunch of disgusting sick people. So apparently the gods were no help at all.

That left the poor—most of the urban population—to die by the thousands. There was no one to bring them even the most basic comforts and no leadership to control the social chaos that might follow in the tracks of the disease.

But the Christians didn't leave. When people became sick, Christians were foolish enough to go to them and help. Sometimes it cost them their lives: We read of more than one bishop who tended to the sick until he himself was struck down by the plague. But sometimes they survived, and so did the people they cared for.

With many of the diseases that tore through the Roman world, the simplest things could make the difference between life and death—bringing water when the patient was too sick to get any for himself, for example. (Remember that there was no running water in the homes of the poor, so getting water meant walking to the nearest source, filling a jar, and hauling the heavy load to where it was needed.) When a patient did get well, he'd remember how kind the Christians had been. He might think that the God who inspired such almost miraculous works of mercy must be very much greater than the pagan gods whose priests were jostling to be first out the city gates.

Julian, the "Pope" of the Pagans

Once Christianity became the favored religion of the empire, its thinking started seeping into the thought of pagans, too. To see how completely Christianity infected the way the world thinks, look no further than the one man who thought he could stamp it out.

The emperor Julian was raised in a Christian family: He was a nephew of the emperor Constantine, who made Christianity the favored religion of the empire. We should say his was a *nominally* Christian family, because they called themselves Christians but acted like monsters. Julian's whole family, except for Julian and a brother named Gallus, was murdered on the orders of his cousin Constantius II, who had come to be emperor and didn't want any possible rivals left alive. (Gallus grew up to become one of the leaders of the Roman world, so Constantius eventually had him executed as well.)

Julian grew up in a nightmarish atmosphere of fear and suspicion, where anyone who seemed like a potential threat to the emperor might suddenly vanish in the middle of the night. And he had to pretend to be happy about it. One of his earliest surviving writings is a panegyric on his murderous cousin Constantius.

Meanwhile, Julian received the best education money could buy, which in those days meant an education in the great philosophers of Greece. So on the one hand, Julian was steeped, if not positively pickled, in the writings of Aristotle and Plato on the subject of the virtuous life; and on the other hand, he was surrounded by self-declared Christians who murdered each other at the drop of a hat. So it's no big surprise that Julian was attracted to the pagan side. When he became emperor he announced that he was a follower of "Hellenism," the old Greek religion of Zeus and Athena and innumerable other deities.

But this Hellenism was not really the old pagan way at all. Julian gave his allegiance to the old gods, but the structure and morality of his revived pagan religion were completely Christian. Julian might rant against the "atheist Galileans," as he contemptuously called Christians, but meanwhile he tried to build a pagan institution that was a mirror image of the Catholic Church.

What made the Church so successful among the masses? It couldn't be Christian doctrine, Julian thought. He was sure that his own philosophical arguments had disproved Christianity conclusively. So it must be the way Christians actually lived their lives.

In his capacity as "pope" of the new paganism, Julian wrote a letter to his head priest in Galatia, in which he ordered him to make sure that the pagan priesthood acted more like Christians. Julian was very specific: Christians have charity, and we don't, and we need to imitate them if we're going to compete. The main barrier to the progress of Julian's peculiar form of pagan puritanism was the fact that Christians came off looking so much better. And that was largely due to Christian charity.

> That Hellenism does not yet succeed as we wish is owing to [the people who profess it]. The gifts of the gods are indeed great and splendid, superior to all our hopes, to all our wishes. For (may Nemesis be propitious to my words!) not long ago no one dared to hope for such a change—and so great a change!—in so short a time. But why should we be satisfied with this, and not rather attend to the means by which this impiety [by which Julian means Christianity] has increased; namely, humanity to strangers, care in burying the dead, and pretended sanctity of life? All these, I think, should be really practiced by us.[4]

Julian didn't believe the Christians were really holier than other people. Remember that his supposedly Christian family was a nest of vipers, so he didn't think much of Christians' claims to special piety. But the point was that *other* people, pagans and Christians, thought the Christians led unusually holy lives. To counter that impression, Julian wanted his priests to be perfectly respectable.

It is not sufficient for you only to be blameless; entreat or compel all the priests that are in Galatia to be also virtuous. If they do not, with their wives, children, and servants, attend the worship of the gods, expel them from the priestly function; and also forbear to converse with the servants, children, and wives of the Galileans [Julian's name for Christians], who are impious towards the gods, and prefer impiety to religion. Admonish also every priest not to frequent the theater, nor to drink in taverns, nor to exercise any trade or employment that is mean and disgraceful. Those who obey you, honor; and those who disobey you, expel. Erect also hospitals in every city, so that strangers may partake our benevolence; and not only those of our own religion, but, if they are indigent, others also.[5]

In other words, the pagan priests should live like Christians. They should do all those things that the Christians had been doing to make their impious atheism so attractive to the common people. This in itself was a victory for Christianity, although Julian didn't realize it. He thought he was a pagan, but his morals were instinctively Christian. The theater, after all, began as a religious celebration, but some of the most religious plays were some of the most obscene. Wine was a gift of the god Bacchus, and drunken revelry had often been a feature of pagan worship.

And now Julian wanted to enforce charity—the idea that had never occurred to classical paganism—by making the pagan priests in every city take in poor strangers the way the Christians did. But how did he think he could pay for that?

How these expenses are to be defrayed must now be considered. I have ordered Galatia to supply you with thirty-thousand bushels of wheat every year; of which the fifth part is to be given to the poor who attend on the priests, and the remainder to be distributed among strangers and our own beggars. For when none of the Jews beg, and the impious Galileans relieve both their own poor and ours, it is shameful that ours should be destitute of our assistance.[6]

Notice how Julian proposed to address the problem. The government would pay for the pagan priests' distributions of food. It's the old Roman idea of philanthropy, trying and failing to compete with Christian charity. The Christians were on the outs with the government and had no resources but their own generosity—yet they still supported the pagan poor as well as the Christian poor. Julian seemed to have no expectation that any such spontaneous outbreak of charity would occur in his new church of pagan fundamentalism.

Julian didn't succeed in restoring paganism, of course. He was killed in battle against the Persians, and the pagan camp had no strong personality to replace him. An old story says that, as Julian fell from his horse, his last words were "You win, Galilean."[7]

But really the Galilean had already won, long before Julian was born. The whole moral revolution that Christ preached is in everything Julian wrote. Intellectually he was a Hellene, but his every instinct was Christian.

Basil and the Eighth Wonder

Contrast Julian's failure with the success of his old friend and schoolmate Basil—the man we now call St. Basil the Great. The two had studied together in Athens, but Basil went on to become a Christian bishop and a doctor of the Church. Basil was the one who really codified the social doctrines of Catholicism. But his wasn't an abstract interest. He was phenomenally successful in exactly the ways Julian failed.

The secret to Basil's success was a combination of deep charity and a brilliant administrative mind. Seeing need everywhere around him in Caesarea, the city where he was bishop, he put together effective ways of helping people in need. There was a soup kitchen for the hungry, poorhouses for the homeless, a trade school for people who needed to find work, a hostel for poor travelers, a nursing home for the old and helpless, and a hospice for the dying. Basil's complex grew so enormous that the astonished citizens of Caesarea began to call it "the new city." His friend St. Gregory of Nazianzus compared the place to the Seven Wonders of the World.

And it was all possible because of charity; it wasn't a government program. Basil's institutions were staffed by Christian ascetics, men and women who freely dedicated themselves to prayer and work. They gave help to anyone who needed it, Christian or not. The money came from donations. Basil told the rich members of his flock that they were investing in their own future. After all, Christ had told them that they would be judged by what they did for the poor (see Matthew 25:31–46). Investing in the poor was investing in heaven.

Basil's "new city" may have been the biggest of the Christian charitable institutions established in the 300s, but it was far from the only one. In fact, Christians set up hospitals, poorhouses, and every other sort of charity all over the place. In every city and town, the poor could find help from a Christian institution. That was why Julian was so worried. What did the pagans have to offer that compared with that?

Fabiola, the Angel of Rome

One of the great heroes of the new charity culture was St. Fabiola, a rich aristocrat who came from one of the leading families in Rome. Married to an abusive husband, she divorced him and remarried—which was legal by Roman law but not by Church law. ("I readily admit that this was a fault," her friend St. Jerome wrote, "but on the other hand I think it might have been a necessity.") When this second husband died, Fabiola made a very public penance. "She laid bare her wound to the gaze of all, and Rome beheld with tears the disfiguring scar which marred her beauty," as Jerome put it.[8] The pope took her back into full communion with the Church.

It soon became clear that Fabiola's penance was more than just a public show. She devoted the rest of her life to study and good works. With her enormous fortune she built a great hospital in Rome, and she worked there herself, tending the worst cases with cheerful love. She patrolled the streets looking for sick people in need of her care and had them brought back to the hospital—or brought them back herself if she had to.

> ...Need I now recount the various ailments of human beings? Need I speak of noses slit, eyes put out, feet half burnt, hands covered with sores? Or of limbs dropsical and atrophied? Or of diseased flesh alive with worms? Often did she carry on her own shoulders persons infected with jaundice or with filth. Often too did she wash away

the matter discharged from wounds which others, even though men, could not bear to look at. She gave food to her patients with her own hand, and moistened the scarce breathing lips of the dying with sips of liquid. I know of many wealthy and devout persons who, unable to overcome their natural repugnance to such sights, perform this work of mercy by the agency of others, giving money instead of personal aid. I do not blame them and am far from construing their weakness of resolution into a want of faith. But while I pardon such squeamishness, I extol to the skies the enthusiastic zeal of a mind that is above it....[9]

Love Never Ends

Charitable institutions were amazing in themselves, but what was even more amazing was the way they survived when every other aspect of civilization was collapsing. Literacy might be a luxury, the roads might decay, the aqueducts might crumble—but Christians still made sure the poor were taken care of. And there were plenty of them to take care of in the miserable ages of wars and invasions that followed the end of Roman power in the West.

When at last the lights began to come on again, there was a new golden age of Christian institutions. Hospitals, orphanages, homes for widows, hostels—many of the earliest charities in Europe—date their foundation to the High Middle Ages. For most of Western history, in fact, the Church has been the main source of help for the poor. It was the same in America: Catholic charity looked after the poor when everyone else was scrambling to make a buck.

Look into your own local history. There's a good chance you'll find that the first hospital in your area was founded by Catholic nuns. Hospitals were rare in America even in the mid–nineteenth century. There was no class of professional nurses to staff them. Only people who had dedicated their lives to service without thought of material reward could afford to work in a hospital.

Today we see the world Christian charity built all around us. How many hospitals are near you? How many nursing homes? Even if they're not Catholic institutions (and many of them are), they all owe the very idea of their existence to Christian charity.

In many ways the government has taken over what used to be the Church's responsibility—making sure that the poor don't starve, that the sick have care. We all agree that something has to be done, that the poor can't just be left to die. But the reason we all agree about that is that Christianity has won. The Christian moral revolution has permeated the thought of the entire world.

When it comes to charity, whether we acknowledge it or not, we're all Christians. Yours is the Church that made that happen.

CHAPTER FOUR

Yours Is the Church That Made Music Great

Mozart—certainly on anyone's short list of the greatest composers in the European tradition—once said that he would gladly trade all his music for the fame of having composed the Gregorian Preface.[1] We should remember that Mozart, who was a Catholic all his life, contributed some of the most famous liturgical music ever written. But he recognized that he was only building on a foundation laid many centuries earlier—the foundation of the Gregorian chant.

It's a long way from medieval plainsong chant to Mozart, but Mozart knew that he stood squarely within the musical tradition that the Church had fostered. More than that, he knew that the support of the Church all through those centuries was really what had made music great.

Many of the brilliant ideas in musical history have come from composers who rebelled against the rules and forms of the previous generation. But "the best traditions make the best rebels," as a famous classical scholar, Gilbert Murray, once said.[2] And one of the glories of the Catholic musical tradition is that it has always found a place for its best rebels.

The basic building blocks of music—the chords, harmonies, and counterpoints that make up a symphony or a popular ballad— grew up in the Church. The Mass was the laboratory of Western music, where composers discovered the principles of melody, polyphony, and harmony.

Music and Worship

Music expresses what words alone can't say. Even in ordinary conversation we use changes of pitch and rhythm to convey how we feel about what we're saying. Music heightens and formalizes those changes, in the same way that poetry heightens and formal- izes the words we speak.

Worship has almost always been musical. Characters of the Old Testament burst into hymns of praise when they were happy and lamentations when they were miserable. Think of the song the Israelites sang after the crossing of the Red Sea (see Exodus 15:1–8) and the Lamentations of Jeremiah after the fall of Jerusalem. The musical part of worship was formalized by David; many pages of the first book of Chronicles are devoted to his arrangements for the liturgical music of the tabernacle service (see 1 Chronicles 25, for example). Psalms is a book of hymns that the people of Israel sang in their worship, both publicly and privately.

Following that Jewish tradition, the early Christians filled their days with psalm singing. Psalms made up an important part of their public worship. And the psalm singing with which they were all familiar influenced the rest of their liturgy.

Melody, Harmony, Polyphony

The more you know about what actually goes on in music, the more you understand how much was happening in those centuries when the only home of serious music—music considered an art form—was the Church. So here's the world's shortest course in music theory.

When you sing a song in the shower, it sounds a lot different from a recording of that same song by your favorite singer. That's only partly because you're not quite as good at singing. It's mostly because there is a lot more going on in the recording than just one person singing.

When you sing in the shower, you sing the *melody*—a string of notes, one after the other, each one set at a particular pitch and held for a particular time. The melody is the basic outline of a song. If you listen to popular songs on the radio, you usually hear that basic outline filled in with a lot of other sounds. For example, there may be backup singers singing along with the lead singer. They're usually singing in *harmony*—that is, they're singing not the melody but notes that go with the melody to make it sound richer and fuller.

Another way to add depth and complexity to music is to have different voices singing different melodies at the same time. Almost everyone has sung "Row, Row, Row Your Boat" as a round: One person starts singing, and then the next starts singing a few beats later. Although they're singing the same melody, they're not singing it at the same time; their voices are going in different directions, but they all fit together. The melodies make different harmonies as they pass each other. That's a simple example of what we call *polyphony:* multiple voices singing different melodies at the same time.

Melody, harmony, polyphony: Along with rhythm, these are the basic building blocks of Western music. They're also three stages in the development of our music.

We start with Gregorian chant, which is pure *melody*. Unlike your song in the shower, it sounds complete even if it's sung by only one voice. Nothing is lacking. Or it can be sung by a group of voices, but they all sing the same notes at the same time.

Sometime in the Middle Ages, perhaps around 900 or so, someone discovered that it sounded very interesting if another voice followed the melody but separated by a *fifth*—five notes on our eight-note scale. Maybe some abbey had a tone-deaf monk in the choir, and the discovery was a lucky accident. If you play the piano at all, try playing a simple melody in fifths. The result is a slightly unearthly sound that's very impressive when it fills a large space, like an abbey church.

This is the most primitive form of *harmony*. Harmony has become so basic to the way we hear music in the West that it's hard for us to realize how unusual it is. In fact, it's almost unique to the European tradition. The only other place that developed a long tradition of harmony was sub-Saharan Africa, where rich harmonies are the norm.

In almost every other musical tradition, harmony is a mistake that happens when somebody hits a wrong note. If you listen to traditional Middle Eastern music, for example, you can hear that it's wonderfully ornate and complex, but it's all melody and rhythm. Even current Middle Eastern pop hits have little if any harmony.

Polyphony is even more complex. Instead of following one another in parallel, the different voices go in different directions. It's like two different chants or songs at once—but they fit together perfectly.

Now, you might think that every note in a polyphonic composition has to be in harmony with the notes sounding at the same time. But that quickly gets cloying. It's like a meal that's all sugar. In fact, composers in the polyphonic style began to develop very strict rules for polyphony. Some notes had to be *dissonant* or the composition wouldn't be pleasant at all.

Notes that are dissonant clash, like colors that just don't go together. If you have a piano, you can try it: Play two notes that are right next to each other. It sounds awful. But those clashes have to be there, like the shadows in a painting, if we're going to hear the light of the harmony.

All these forms of music—melody, harmony, polyphony—reached their high point as art in the service of the Church.

The Mass as Art

Everything in music—not just everything in Church music, but everything in the Western musical tradition—starts with Gregorian chant. It's melody in its purest form, simple yet capable of infinite variation.

No one knows exactly how Gregorian chant developed. Even the name is obscure. An old tradition says that Pope Gregory the Great gathered together and systematized the Church's liturgical music as part of his great liturgical reform in about 600; but tradition may have confused him with the much less famous Gregory II, who came about two centuries later. At any rate, it's clear that what we call Gregorian chant came from the codification of traditional "plainsong" chants that were in use in various parts of Western Europe.

The Catholic Church still considers Gregorian chant the norm for liturgical music. But in the later Middle Ages, the new polyphonic style of composition attracted the attention of some of the best musicians of the day. They called their style *Ars Nova*—the "New Art." There was actually some considerable debate about whether polyphony could ever be suitable for liturgical music, but the new generation of composers worked very hard to show that it could be dignified, spiritual, and beautiful. In about 1360 Guillaume de Machaut, the greatest composer of the *Ars Nova,* wrote the first complete polyphonic Mass, the Mass of Our Lady *(Messe de Nostre Dame).*

Why did these composers care so much whether polyphony was allowed in the Church? Because the Mass, itself one of the great works of art, is an irresistible subject for a composer. Every mood of the human spirit is there, waiting to be set to music. Our most exalted thoughts are waiting for someone to sing them.

Wolfgang Amadeus Mozart was a child prodigy, as everyone knows. But his father, even though he encouraged the boy genius's musical career, always put the faith first. And Mozart himself grew into a faithful Catholic who enriched the Church with a huge library of sacred music. Mozart has left us no fewer than sixteen Mass Ordinary settings, and his two greatest choral masterpieces are both unfinished.

In the first of these, *The Mass in C Minor,* Mozart very consciously placed himself in the long tradition of sacred music, deliberately imitating and making reference to the works of his predecessors. But of course it's all Mozart, instantly recognizable as his work.

The other of his greatest sacred works is the *Requiem.* You'll find plenty of critics who are prepared to say that—even in its unfinished and somewhat mutilated state—Mozart's *Requiem* is the greatest choral work of all time. The poignant irony of the story that goes with it makes it a favorite of music teachers: Mozart began work on a Requiem Mass he had been commissioned to compose, only to realize as he got into the work, and his health deteriorated, that he was writing his own requiem.

Ludwig van Beethoven is the face of classical music in popular culture. His intensity, his passion, and his disregard for inconvenient rules of composition have defined the popular image of the musical artist. In many ways he picked up in music where Mozart left off. And again, Beethoven found some of his deepest inspiration in the Catholic liturgy. His *Missa Solemnis* (Solemn Mass) stands beside Bach's *Mass in B minor* and Mozart's *Requiem* at the peak of choral music in the Western tradition.

Even composers outside the Catholic tradition found some of their greatest inspirations in Catholic liturgy. Johann Sebastian Bach was a Lutheran all his life—but of all his choral works, the *Mass in B minor*, which he wrote for the King of Poland, is probably his masterpiece. It isn't the work of a hack writing whatever his patron wants: It's the profound expression of a brilliant mind coming face-to-face with eternal truth.

Adventures of a Medieval Hymn

Aside from the fact that all the techniques of Western musical composition developed in sacred music, music's debt to the Catholic Church goes deeper. The Catholic liturgy inspired more than just musical settings of the Mass. A look at the works of the great composers shows liturgical music popping up all over the place.

For just one example, let's take the *Dies Irae*, a hymn written in the 1200s, probably by the Franciscan friar Thomas of Celano.

It became part of the Requiem Mass, and so it came to be a sort of musical shorthand for death. You may not know the hymn, but you've certainly heard it, whether in symphonies or cartoon soundtracks. It's the basis of Saint-Saens's *Danse Macabre* and also a main theme in his *Organ Symphony*. The great Russian composer Sergei Rachmaninoff was so obsessed with the melody that he worked it into almost every major composition he published. But that's just a start.

Haydn used it in his *Symphony No. 103*.
Berlioz used it in his *Symphonie Fantastique*.
Gounod used it in his opera *Faust*.
Liszt used it in his *Totentanz* ("Death Dance").
Tchaikovsky used it in his *Manfred Symphony*.
Mahler used it in his *Symphony No. 2*.
Holst used it in *The Planets*.
Shostakovich used it in his *Symphony No. 13*.
Stephen Sondheim used it in the musical *Sweeney Todd*.
The contemporary composer Michael Daugherty used it
in his *Metropolis Symphony*, which is based on the adventures of Superman.

And that is just a tiny smattering of the musical compositions—not counting actual Requiem Masses—in which the *Dies Irae* is a prominent theme.

Many of these composers weren't Catholic or even religious. But when they came to confront the mystery of death, this was the music that popped into their heads. Even for people who have never heard the hymn in the context of the Requiem Mass, the melody has a powerful resonance as the instantly recognizable sound of doom. And in spite of the enormous changes in music in the past century, the *Dies Irae* still haunts the imaginations of contemporary composers. Sometimes it seems to be the only constant in the ever-changing landscape of Western music.

Even when that musical landscape is changing the most, we find that the tradition of the Church is behind some of the great works in the newest styles. For example, what could be more non-European, newer, or more different than jazz? Yet the first lady of jazz, Mary Lou Williams, turned to the Catholic Church to find the inspiration jazz alone wasn't giving her.

Mary Lou Williams

Mary Lou Williams grew up in Pittsburgh at a time when the city's African American neighborhoods were famous for their thriving musical culture. Like Mozart, she was a child prodigy. By the age of seven, she was already earning a reputation around town as a pianist. Before she was twenty, she had joined Andy Kirk and His Clouds of Joy, a Kansas City band that was just beginning to make a national reputation for itself.

With Kirk's band Williams quickly showed a talent for writing music as well as playing it. At a time when there were almost no female jazz musicians, Williams had the respect and admiration of the biggest names in the field. She was billed as "The Lady Who Swings the Band," and within a few years the top names in popular music were playing her music—Benny Goodman, Earl Hines (another Pittsburgh native), Tommy Dorsey, and Duke Ellington, to name a few.

Williams was on the cutting edge of jazz. Up-and-coming stars such as Dizzy Gillespie made pilgrimages to her apartment to hear her play and jam with her. Her reputation continued to grow, and in the early 1950s she went to Europe to play for fans who had only heard her on records until then.

But in the middle 1950s, the flow of records suddenly stopped, and Williams wasn't showing up at nightclubs anymore. What had happened? In fact, that stay in Europe had changed her. Now she was looking for something more than fame and success.

In spite of her reputation among the giants of jazz, Williams had always had a hard time making a living with her music. She had an enormous family back in Pittsburgh who were worse off than she was, and she could never resist helping them out. In fact, the Pittsburgh relatives always assumed she was rich. Didn't they hear her on the radio all the time? Weren't her records in all the stores? And wasn't she always sending them money? They had no idea how little she had left for herself.

Worse yet, while she was in Paris, alone and thousands of miles away from everyone she knew, she began to feel as though her music wasn't doing anything for her. It wasn't just that she couldn't make enough money; the music wasn't satisfying her spirit.

One day, one of her Paris friends—an expatriate American who happened to be a Catholic—took her to a little city church with a walled garden. And in that garden, she recounted later, she found God.

But what had she really found? She didn't know. She started to pray every day, and she often found herself reading the Psalms. But she was still looking—still trying to figure out what this new discovery meant in her life.

When she came back to New York, she intensified her spiritual search. She tried going to a Baptist church for a while, but that wasn't what she was looking for. She made lists of hundreds of people to pray for, and she would spend hours in prayer every day. Meanwhile, though she wasn't bringing in any money, she supported indigent family members who showed up on her doorstep, some of whom had destructive drug habits and simply couldn't take care of themselves.

She couldn't stand the atmosphere of the nightclubs anymore, where it seemed that people didn't care about their own souls. She was thinking of leaving music altogether. But then her friend Dizzy Gillespie introduced her to a friend of his—a Jesuit priest, the Rev. Anthony Woods. He had a different suggestion. Offer your music up as a prayer for others, he told her.

Suddenly things began to make sense. Her musical gifts were something good; they weren't a distraction from her real vocation. In fact, her real vocation was to lead people to God through music.

In 1957 Mary Lou Williams was baptized in the Catholic Church. Now she began the new phase of her career—one that would probably have astonished the people who knew her as "The Lady Who Swings the Band" in the 1930s. She began to write sacred music—but sacred music in the jazz idiom. Her first substantial religious work had a text by Fr. Woods: *Black Christ of the Andes* (Hymn in Honor of St. Martin of Porres).

One might expect that the jazz world would have turned its collective back on Mary Lou Williams. After all, jazz musicians aren't always known for their exemplary religious lives. But in fact the new music was a sensation. Williams's new album, *Mary*

Lou Williams Presents St. Martin of Porres, won all sorts of prestigious awards.

Her next big project was even bigger and (at least at the time) completely unique: a jazz Mass. *Mary Lou's Mass* was built from the long tradition of spirituals in the South, the European tradition of artistic settings of the Mass—like Mozart's, Beethoven's, and Verdi's—and the still-evolving tradition of jazz. The commission for the Mass came from the Vatican, and the Mass was performed for the first time at St. Patrick Cathedral in New York.

The Music of the Future

We've seen that, in the history of music, innovation and creation were driven by the Catholic Church. The enthralling spell of the Mass, with its deep emotions and lofty thoughts, has inspired some of the greatest music, from Gregorian chant to jazz. And what about the future of music?

No one can make predictions with any certainty. But we do know that the great Catholic tradition in music is as fascinating now to musicians and composers—and to the public at large—as it ever was. Who would have guessed that albums of chanting monks would climb to the top of the charts? Yet millions of people who would never call themselves Catholic embraced this pure and ancient Catholic liturgical music, and record companies fell over each other to sign abbey choirs for their catalogs.

That enormous revival of interest in Gregorian chant over the last few decades has probably influenced the coming generation of musicians. Likewise the huge revival of baroque and "early music." It's safe to say that the musicians of tomorrow are still growing up in the Catholic tradition, which they may not even recognize as Catholic. But as its riches open up to them, they'll be more and more enthralled by it. And many of them will be led by the music back to the welcoming arms of their mother the Church.

CHAPTER FIVE

Yours Is the Church That Inspired the Great Works of Art

What's the greatest painting of all time? Is it Leonardo da Vinci's *Last Supper?* Or Michelangelo's Sistine Chapel ceiling?

What about the greatest sculpture? Is it Michelangelo's *David?* Or his *Pieta?*

Are you seeing a trend here? When we think of great art, we think of art and artists who have been fostered and inspired by the Catholic Church.

We don't want to make the mistake of canonizing our great artists; we know they were sinners. But when we see the greatest talents in the history of art seized by an idea and producing their greatest masterpieces under its spell, then we've got to say that it must be a very powerful idea. The Incarnation is a powerful idea—so powerful that it has captured the imaginations of countless artists from every continent.

Michelangelo, Leonardo, Raphael—these were artists to whom every door was open, who painted every subject. But the most unforgettable monuments to their genius are their religious works. This fact is significant not just because people were willing to pay the artists to create these works but because that divine fire that artists call "inspiration"—itself an idea taken from Christian thought—shines brightly through them.

The Right to Make Pictures

We very nearly didn't have art at all—or at least we very nearly didn't have that glorious tradition of representational art of which we're so proud today. More than once, the ugly specter of iconoclasm cast its dark shadow over Europe.

Iconoclasm means "image smashing." In the West it almost always comes from a stern and severe interpretation of one of the Ten Commandments: "You shall not make for yourself a graven image, or any likeness of anything that is in heaven above, or that is in the earth beneath, or that is in the water under the earth; you shall not bow down to them or serve them" (Exodus 20:4–5).

Now, there are broadly two ways of interpreting this commandment. The first way, which is the way the Catholic Church interprets it, is that we may not make idols: that is, we may not make images for the purpose of worshiping them. The other way of understanding it is that we may not make images at all, for any purposes whatsoever. You can see how that would cramp the development of art.

Some forms of Judaism and some forms of Islam have concluded that all images are prohibited, at least all images of people and animals. In parts of the Islamic world where this prohibition is taken most seriously, there is a rich tradition of decorative art that uses fantastically intricate patterns from the vegetable kingdom and gorgeous calligraphy that weaves verses from the Koran into astonishing ornaments. But there is no art that tells stories, and there are certainly no portraits, either of current notables or of great figures of the past.

Christians have often been tempted toward that kind of severity, and sometimes that has erupted in terrible destruction. The first was in the time of Leo the Isaurian. Leo III became Roman emperor (we'd say "Byzantine emperor" today) in 717, at a time when the Eastern Roman Empire was in real danger of falling apart. Islamic conquerors had overrun more than half the empire, and the rest was hanging by a thread. Now the caliph was besieging Constantinople itself, the capital and the greatest city in Christendom.

With quick action, acute political skill, and great personal courage, Leo managed to get the empire back on its feet so well that it held on for another seven centuries. And if that had been the end of his accomplishments, we might remember him as at least the greatest emperor since Justinian. But Leo, who was decisive in everything, had strong opinions about religion. Perhaps because he came from the far east of the empire, where he was surrounded by Islamic and Jewish thought, he had come to the conclusion that the almost universal Christian practice of venerating icons— pictures of saints and of Christ—was a form of idolatry. And it was his duty, as the head of the Christian Empire, to stamp it out. The patriarch of Constantinople resigned in protest, but Leo just found another patriarch who was more pliable.

A few of the images were squirreled away in inaccessible monasteries or hidden in secret caves, but far more were burned or smashed to splinters. Some of the faithful were willing to endure torture or death rather than give up their precious icons. For his part, Leo was perfectly willing to torture and kill. The destruction and persecution reminded the people who lived through it of the martyrs in the great pagan persecutions.

Except in the small part of Italy that was directly under Byzantine control, this outbreak of fanaticism never really reached Western Europe—and that Byzantine part of Italy rebelled. Most of the West seems to have felt that the emperor of the East had simply flipped his lid. But it took another Easterner, John of Damascus, to articulate the truly Catholic argument for the use of images in the Church. In the end, the Second Council of Nicea accepted his position that European art could be representational, not just strictly geometric or decorative.

To make our confession short: We keep unchanged all the traditions of the Church handed down to us, whether in writing or by word of mouth. One of these is the making of pictorial representations, which fits with the history of the preaching of the Gospel. The tradition is useful in many ways, but especially in this: that by it the incarnation of the Word of God is shown as real, and not merely a fantasy.[1]

Yours is the Church that made Western art possible. And European artists repaid their debt by dedicating their lives to the service of your Church.

The Cathedral

Walk into any of the great Gothic cathedrals, and you'll see instantly how much art meant to the faithful people who built them. Today we might put up a building and then find a little space in one corner of the lobby for a work of art. But that way of doing things would simply baffle a medieval architect. In a Gothic cathedral every square inch is art. And all the arts come together in a wonderfully Catholic way.

The architect maps out the shape of the cathedral. Sculptors not only adorn it with statues but actually shape all the pieces of the building—the columns, the beams, the furnishings, even the humblest practical accessories. Artists in stained glass fill the windows with glowing images. Where there is a blank wall, painters cover it with pictures from Scripture or the lives of the saints or visions of the heavenly kingdom. The organ is a magnificent work of art. The vestments are gorgeously embroidered. The setting is appropriate for the liturgy, which is itself one of the greatest works of art, a poetic drama in which the story of our salvation unfolds before us.

Art is not something that adds decoration to religious life. Art is the way religious life is lived. When you enter a medieval church, you walk into a world where life and art are inseparable. This is the world in which the great artists of the Middle Ages and the Renaissance grew up. It shaped their ideas not only of what art should look like but of what art should be.

The Renaissance

What we call the Renaissance was the direct result of that same revival of ancient learning that inspired the deep thoughts of Thomas Aquinas and Albert the Great. Artists and architects turned to the surviving examples of ancient art and building for their inspiration—but they turned their new skills to Christian themes.

It's a commonplace that the Church had become very worldly at the time of the Renaissance, and there's more than a little truth in that commonplace. The papacy was recruited from the powerful political families of Italy—people like the Borgias and the Medicis, who were not known for their saintly morals. Cardinals and bishops often rose to their positions because of their wealth and then used their positions to accumulate more wealth.

But *worldly* is not the word to describe the art left to us by people like Michelangelo and Raphael. These artists gave us works that the whole world recognizes as the apex of Western art. And for all the damage the "worldly" popes may have done, we have to wonder whether the world hasn't benefited more from their patronage than it suffered from their corruption.

These artists weren't just great painters and sculptors; they were revolutionaries in their time. It might have been easy for the more reactionary to think that what they were doing wasn't suitable for religious art at all. Compare, for example, the art of Eastern Christianity—a glorious tradition of icons, painted with extraordinary skill and delicacy, conveying a profound sense of the divine, but almost unchanged in a millennium and a half. Why wasn't Western art frozen the same way? Is it because the popes of the Renaissance were worldly? If that was the price we had to pay for Michelangelo, it was probably worth paying.

Michelangelo is one of the great characters in art as well as one of the great artists. He was a deeply religious man. He never married, and some recent art historians have tried to portray him as a homosexual. But his contemporaries seem to have thought of him as more like a monk. He had committed himself to God, in fact, as a Third Order Franciscan. When he started a project, he worked on it obsessively, ignoring everything else in his life—unless he thought his dignity as an artist had been insulted. Then he could instantly turn into a spoiled child.

When Michelangelo was working on sculptures for the new Basilica of St. Peter, he went to Pope Julius to ask for money for the marble, which he had paid for out of his own pocket. The pope's servants refused to admit him, saying the pope was busy. Michelangelo stomped away, sold his belongings, left Rome, and wouldn't come back until he was practically dragged there. But the pope forgave him, because in all the world there was only one Michelangelo.

When it came to the Sistine Chapel, his greatest work as a painter, Michelangelo approached the project in typical fashion. At first he sent for some competent artists he knew in Florence to fill in the colors of his designs, but he took one look at their first efforts and locked them out of the chapel, erasing everything they had done and starting over. For nearly two years he worked alone, on scaffolding he designed himself.

When the project was finally unveiled, it was so impressive that Raphael, Michelangelo's unfriendly rival, paid the artist the greatest possible tribute. According to the biographer Vasari, who knew both of them, "Raphael, who was excellent in imitating, at once changed his style after seeing it."[2]

Michelangelo and Raphael are only the tip of the iceberg. The Renaissance was probably the most glorious age in the history of painting, and Christian subjects dominate the lists of all the artists' best-known works.

Leonardo da Vinci—there's a name to reckon with among painters. His *Mona Lisa* is not an explicitly religious work—but it's in the minority. Think of his *Last Supper* and his *Madonna of the Rocks*.

Or how about Tintoretto? He gave us no fewer than eight versions of the *Last Supper*.

Veronese gave us *The Finding of Moses* and *The Marriage Feast at Cana.*

Correggio gave us *Noli Me Tangere* (a depiction of Jesus's encounter with Mary Magdalene after the Resurrection) and an astonishing *Assumption of the Virgin* in the dome of the cathedral at Parma.

Perugino painted a famous *Crucifixion* and *Christ Giving the Keys to St. Peter.*

It was the patronage of the Church that made these great works possible. But it was not patronage that made them great. The painters were seized by the wonderful stories and ideas of the Catholic faith—ideas that simply demanded to be painted.

More than one of these great painters had to fight with the bishop or cardinal who had commissioned him in order to win the right to paint the subject the way he saw it—the way it had taken control of his imagination. But the battle was worth fighting because the subject had gotten under his skin. He simply couldn't fathom *not* painting it the way he imagined it.

From Then to Now

Art didn't end with the Renaissance, of course. As we move on into the Baroque period, we still find religious subjects inspiring the great works—Carracci's *Lamentation of Christ,* Caravaggio's *Supper at Emmaus,* Poussin's *Gathering of Manna.* Even in later eras, when secular patrons had more money and were able to compete successfully for the attention of the best artists of the time, we still find that some of the most memorable paintings are religious subjects.

The twentieth century saw enormous changes in the whole idea of art. Some people thought art had lost its mind or perhaps its heart. Yet even then, the long tradition of Christian religious art wasn't dead. It was still alive, hidden away in some unexpected places.

The world remembers Andy Warhol's wild parties, his paintings of Hollywood celebrities and soup cans, his elevation of consumer culture to high art. But under all the layers of gaudy cultural pretension, Andy Warhol could never shake off his Byzantine Catholic roots. He was obsessed with religious iconography, especially in his last years.

More than that, Warhol had become secretly religious himself. He attended the Divine Liturgy every week at a Byzantine church, though none of his friends knew about it. When he died, his body came back to his native Pittsburgh for a Byzantine Catholic funeral.

Warhol's papers and much of his art came back to Pittsburgh too, where they're kept in the largest museum in the country (possibly the world) dedicated to a single artist. Among his effects were hundreds of paintings and drawings of religious subjects. He did more than a hundred paintings of the Last Supper alone, each exploring a different aspect of Leonardo's famous masterpiece. It turned out that Andy Warhol had been a Catholic—and a devout one in his own way—all the time we thought he was worshiping a Campbell's soup can.

But even when art isn't explicitly religious, we find that the Catholic tradition is guiding it, often in ways the artists themselves don't recognize. In every generation artists rebel against the ordinariness of life. They dream of a world where everything is artistic, where—just as in the great cathedrals—even the humblest appliance is a masterpiece of design. The Arts and Crafts movement of the 1800s, the Bauhaus in the 1920s, the modernists of the 1960s, the postmodernists and the post-postmodernists— they're all dreaming of that world of truly Catholic art, where all that meets the eye is artistic. It's a world we know can really exist, because it does exist in the Gothic cathedrals.

CHAPTER SIX

Yours Is the Church That Inspired Great Literature

Pagan literature was a glorious thing once. Homer, Sophocles, Virgil, Cicero—these names will live as long as people read books. But by the time Constantine made Christianity legal, it was pretty much all over.

That doesn't mean no one was writing anything. It just means no one was writing anything worth reading. Pagan literature had run out of things to say. In fact, it had stopped trying to say anything.

By about the year 300, literature was into reruns. A writer earned praise not for what he had to say but for imitating the styles of certain approved authors as closely as possible. Saying something original actually put a writer at a disadvantage. How could one know how Cicero would have said it if Cicero had never written anything on the topic?

Often the recycling went further than mere imitation. One of the popular literary forms of the day was the *cento*, a poem made up entirely of lines from other poems. For example, someone might write a new poem by taking lines here and there from *The Iliad* and fitting them together in a new order. This took incredible skill and an encyclopedic memory. But the whole point was to avoid saying anything new.

Many Christians grew up with the same education as their pagan neighbors, and they wrote in the same artificial style. But the best of the Christian writers had something to say. And if it took inventing a whole new form of literature to say it, then that was what they would do.

St. Augustine Confesses

The list of great writers from the 300s and 400s is almost entirely populated by Christians. There was St. John Chrysostom, whose sermons were so memorable that they became the chief public entertainment in Constantinople, earning him his nickname "Golden-Mouthed" (that's what *Chrysostom* means). There was St. Jerome, notoriously crusty but brilliant, who translated the Bible from the original languages into Latin, creating the version we still use as the official Catholic standard. He also found time to write letters we still look to as models of elegant correspondence.

But of all the people writing at that time, the most influential was St. Augustine. His theological works were so brilliant that St. Jerome claimed he "established the old faith anew."[1] If we had nothing but his letters and his treatises on theology, we would count him as one of the titans of literature. But we also have one work of his that has earned a place as one of the most admired books of all time—the first real autobiography.

Written in the form of a long confession to God, the *Confessions* is the story of St. Augustine's life from the inside. Nothing like it had ever appeared before, and probably nothing like it will ever appear again.

Plenty of pagan writers had written down the stories of their own brilliant accomplishments. There was a time not long ago when every schoolchild had to struggle through Julius Caesar's *Gallic War* in second-year Latin, learning along the way that Gaul was divided into three parts. There was much grumbling that the whole thing might have been more interesting if Caesar hadn't insisted on referring to himself in the third person.

But no one had ever taken his own life and dissected it with the minute attention of a scientist studying the anatomy of a fish. No one had ever been so ruthlessly honest about his own failings. (In fact, if you read Caesar, you might be forgiven for thinking that the man had never made a mistake in his life.)

What was new was the Christian idea of sin. It was oddly liberating: St. Augustine, Bishop of Hippo in the province of Africa, didn't have to pretend that he was always perfect, because Christians already knew that no one was free from sin. He examined his thoughts, even those from the beginning of his life, with extraordinary minuteness:

> Hear me, O God: Woe to the sins of men—and a man says this, and you have mercy on him, because you made him but did not make sin in him.
>
> Who will give me an account of the sin of my infancy? Since no one is pure from sin in your sight, not even the infant that is but a day old [a reference to Job 25], who will give me an account? Shall it be another little one, in whom I now see what I don't remember of myself?
>
> What then was my sin at that time? Was it crying greedily after the breast? For if I should at present thus greedily hang over, not the breasts, but the food that suits

70

my age, I should most justly be derided and reprehended. Therefore at that time I did what deserved reprehension, but because I could not understand reproof, neither custom nor reason allowed me to be reproved; for as we grow up we pluck up and cast these things away.

Now, no one who is cleansing anything willingly casts away that which is good. Or was it good in that age to demand with tears what would have been hurtful if granted—to rage and swell against those that owed me no subjection, against my betters, and my very parents; and to strive by striking at them to hurt those that were far wiser than I was for not complying with my will, and obeying my commands, which it would have been hurtful to have obeyed?

So it's the weakness of infants' limbs and not their inclination that is innocent. I myself have seen and had experience of such a little one already possessed with jealousy; it had not learned to speak, and yet it would cast a pale and envious look at its fellow suckling. Is there anyone not familiar with this? And mothers and nurses say they expiate these things with I know not what remedies.

In the meantime can I call this innocence, if one who is very rich in a fountain of milk that flows plentifully, and even overflows, cannot even endure to let another partake a little with him—and that one another that is not able to provide for himself, and that can sustain life only with this food?

But such things as these are lovingly borne, not because they are not evils, or only small evils, but because they will go away as age comes on. However much they are at that time allowed, they would not be tolerated when discovered in riper years.[2]

Has any other writer ever taken a microscope to his own infancy in that way? Most of us would simply dismiss the idea, but St. Augustine dove right in, using what he saw in infants around him to imagine what he must have been like.

His *Confessions* is a startlingly modern work. Not until the twentieth century would writers consistently try to imitate Augustine's objective self-examination—and even then, there's no one who did it as well. Measured by the crassest possible standard, St. Augustine beats them all: He still sells more copies than all those other writers. Right now there are dozens of editions of the *Confessions* in print just in English, not to mention the languages of the rest of the world. And that's not counting e-books.

The *Confessions* is the story of Augustine's own conversion. It blasted a hole right through all the categories of classical literature, because it said something that no one had ever said before. St. Augustine created his own category and sent literature reeling in a new direction.

And because Augustine reached so deeply into his own soul, we can see the depths of our souls in his work as well. The book is still making conversions today, sixteen centuries later.

Light in the Darkness

We've already seen how hard the Dark Ages fell across Western Europe—literacy was practically wiped out in less than a century. But here and there we see sparks of genius even in the deepest darkness. And when we do see them, they're always in the Church.

There simply wasn't a place for literature anywhere else.

The Venerable Bede is one of the brightest of those sparks. An English monk in Northumbria, he was extraordinarily well educated for his time. He knew Greek as well as Latin, making him one of the relatively few Greek scholars in Western Europe. He made translations of some of the Greek fathers of the Church. He also wrote important works on theology.

Bede's greatest effort was his *Ecclesiastical History of the English Nation*, the first history of England, which he finished in 731. Bede's wide reading shows: His Latin style is comparable to some of the best writing in classical times, and he organized his history intelligently and told his stories engagingly. It's a work of history that would have been exceptional in any era; in the depths of the Dark Ages, it was simply astonishing.

Charlemagne's revival of classical learning brought out a number of exceptionally good writers, of whom perhaps the best was his close friend Eginhard or Einhard, who wrote a *Life of Charlemagne* that rivals the best classical biographies of great men. Eginhard was educated in a monastery, though he was not a monk. In fact he married, although he and his wife devoted their later years to married celibacy.

Later, of course, we come to the age of Albert the Great and Thomas Aquinas, when some of the deepest thoughts ever thought were being expressed in language that's a model of clarity for philosophers attacking difficult questions. We've talked about the influence of Thomas Aquinas on philosophy and science, but it's worth mentioning here that he was a master of explanatory prose and profound liturgical poetry as well.

So far all the literature in Western Europe, with few exceptions, had been produced within the Church or by people closely associated with the Church. But perhaps it is even more interesting to see what happened when secular literature began to compete for attention.

Medieval Romance

As the high Middle Ages went on, more and more people outside the Church were learning to read. The nobility were expected to be literate, which created a large demand for secular literature for the first time in seven hundred years. Ancient folk tales were written down, embellished, reworked, and turned into entertainments for the courts of the innumerable princes, dukes, and counts who governed Europe at the time.

Naturally, these entertainments tended to reflect the debauched morals of their audiences in the upper classes. They were love stories, and to noble knights and ladies of that time, love and marriage were two entirely separate subjects. In fact, it was pretty much assumed that love had to be adulterous. The heroine's husband was some ogre her father had forced on her; the love of her life was a handsome knight whom she met sometime after her unhappy marriage. Some of the stories were tragic: The lovers would be killed together, commit suicide, or come to some other romantic tearjerker of an end. But sometimes there was a "happy" ending: The handsome knight would kill the ogre husband and live happily ever after with his wife.

Of all the medieval romances, none were more popular than the tales of King Arthur's court. And of all the famous pairs of lovers in romance, none were more famous than Lancelot and Guinevere. The story of their adulterous love is still one of our favorite entertainments. But of course it does involve pretty much all the mortal sins. It was not a good model for a nobility that had already absorbed the idea that adulterous love was the greatest thing ever.

It took an audaciously daring and even perverse mind to make that story into a religious allegory, but that's exactly what some unknown cleric—or group of clerics—decided to do. As we know it from its most famous incarnation, the Arthurian romance of Lancelot and Guinevere and the story of the Holy Grail that goes with it are a profound allegory of sin and redemption. By his sin Lancelot destroys the earthly paradise of Camelot. But he is not irredeemable: His visions of the Holy Grail lead him on the diffi-cult path to repentance. He cannot really achieve his redemption until he learns that everything he thought was glorious—the chiv-alry, the love of Guinevere, his own boldness in battle—was sin.

It was a daring message to preach to a nobility that admired Lancelot as the summation of everything good in the world. But the story was so artistically told that it drew its audience in. People didn't realize they were being taught the most orthodox Catholic theology of sin and repentance. They couldn't get enough of the story, and so they absorbed a message that they wouldn't have taken from any fire-and-brimstone preacher in a pulpit.

This is a story so memorable that every generation tells it again, in novels, in movies, and on television. And no matter how much Hollywood tries to dilute the message, it still peeks through.

Dante

The medieval genius for seeing the truth in an allegory was behind another great work, perhaps the single greatest work of literature between the fall of Rome in the West and the Renaissance.

Dante Alighieri was born in Florence in 1265. He dabbled in poetry, but he probably had a political career in mind, and he was off to a good start when the tawdry politics of medieval Florence erupted in spectacular violence. Dante was away in Rome on a diplomatic mission at the time, and in his absence he was sentenced to exile for the crime of belonging to the losing party. He was sentenced to be burned at the stake if he ever came back. (Florence rescinded his sentence in 2008, by which time Dante wasn't worrying about it very much.)

Exiled from his home, stripped of his property, and barred from politics, Dante had nowhere to turn his talents but to his poetry. In 1308 he began work on a poem that would occupy him for more than a decade, right up to the time of his death in 1321. Dante simply called it the *Commedia* or "Comedy." (He meant *comedy* in the original sense of a work with a happy ending, not in the sense of a play with a laugh track.) It was Boccaccio, another great Italian writer, who first called the work the *Divina Commedia,* or "Divine Comedy."

Dante was familiar with the works of our old friend Thomas Aquinas, and the idea had entered his head that he could somehow encapsulate the sum of Catholic theology in an allegorical vision. Everything about the work is in threes. There are three parts, telling of Dante's journey through hell, purgatory, and paradise. The verse itself is in *terza rima*, three-part rhyme, in which the first and third lines always rhyme with the middle line of the previous group, so that the rhyme seems to be woven all the way through the work:

In just about the middle of life's way,
I found myself caught in a forest drear,

And could not tell which way the right road lay.

Never before did such a wood appear
To me, impenetrable, savage, dense—
The very thought of it brings back my fear.[3]

And so on.

Dante couldn't resist putting some of his enemies in hell and the love of his life in heaven. But the profound allegory of death and resurrection, sin and salvation, expressed in the structure as well as the words of the poem, transcends any pettiness.

Perhaps the most daring thing about the poem was the language in which it was written. In those days all educated discourse was written in Latin. French was beginning to come into its own as a literary language, and the great Arthurian romances had been written in French. But there was no such thing as Italian; there was only a confusion of dialects descended from Latin, somewhat but not completely intelligible to each other. Dante (who wrote in very elegant Latin when he had a mind to do it) decided to write his greatest work in the Tuscan dialect, the everyday language of Florence.

To make a poem out of the *Summa Theologica* was audacious enough. To make a poem in which the structure was as much an expression of the idea as the words were was the work of a genius. But to write it all in a dialect that had never been a vehicle for serious literature before must have seemed almost mad. Yet in Dante's skilled hands, this Florentine dialect was suddenly an elegant literary language. In fact, modern Italians regard Dante as the father of their tongue. His Florentine dialect became the standard language for the whole peninsula and is the current language of newspapers, novels, and laws in the Republic of Italy.

The poem itself belongs to the world, not just to Italy. It has inspired innumerable works of art, including a series of stunning illustrations by Gustave Doré and the tone poem *Francesca da Rimini* by Tchaikovsky. It has been translated into English many times, including once by the great twentieth-century writer Dorothy Sayers, who preserved the unique rhyme scheme in English.

Cervantes

The greatest name in Spanish literature, on the other hand, never set out to make a profound allegory and didn't worry much about structures and forms. He just wanted to tell a good story and have a good laugh. It seems pure accident that he ended up writing what is almost universally acknowledged as the greatest novel in history.

Don Quixote started out as a parody of chivalric romances. The story is simple: A gentleman whose mind is addled from too much reading of silly romances begins to fancy himself a knight in shining armor, and he sallies out to have a bunch of ridiculous adventures. The real world laughs at the old madman and his absurd fantasy. But as we read, we begin to wonder whether the real world is not mad and the crazy old knight the only sane man in it.

Somehow Cervantes manages to have it both ways: He laughs at his hero and makes us laugh with him, but we also grow to love and admire Don Quixote. We begin to think that it must be a glorious thing to be as mad as he is.

The whole story takes place in a Catholic world—not just because it takes place in a Catholic country but because it depends on a Catholic way of seeing humanity. We are fallen and imperfect, but we are also great, created in the image of God. When we are at our most ridiculous is perhaps when there is the most hope for us.

Don Quixote is a fool, but he is a holy fool. He believes that the world can be made better by one person—and because he believes it, it actually starts to happen. This is how a Catholic lives life in this world of sin: constantly tilting at windmills, with the faith to believe that dragons will be slain if we only stick to the battle.

English Catholic Literature

We could say that English literature—at least literature in a language we'd recognize as English—begins with Chaucer. His *Canterbury Tales* are steeped in Catholic culture.

The premise involves a pilgrimage to the shrine of St. Thomas à Becket in Canterbury. Along the way we meet saints and sinners; we hear silly stories and vulgar tales, an improving sermon or two, and some doggerel rhyme that Chaucer puts into his own mouth as a kind of in-joke for the reader. The very variety of the work is Catholic: There is hope for the sinners, and even the saints are refreshingly human.

Of course, most people would say that the biggest name in English literature is William Shakespeare, who wrote after Queen Elizabeth had made the final break with Rome and declared herself head of the Church of England. Was Shakespeare Catholic? One intriguing theory suggests that he was, but it's only guesswork.

The fact is that, even if he was Church of England through and through, Shakespeare had thoroughly Catholic sensibilities. His plays expressed better than anyone else's the way the ordinary Englishman in the street felt. And ordinary English people didn't stop being Catholic just because Queen Elizabeth told them to. Yes, they may have been going to the official parish church. They may have taken an oath of loyalty to the queen as head of the church. But they had Catholic habits of thought. You can't erase a thousand years' worth of ingrained ideas in a single generation.

That's why it may always be impossible to tell whether Shakespeare was actually a Catholic. England was Catholic in all its thinking; it would take generations before there could be any real separation between Anglican and Catholic thinking in the ordinary English mind.

We do know that one of the greatest English poets after Shakespeare was Catholic. He bore the suggestive name Alexander Pope, and he practically defined English poetry for the 1700s. Even today, his translation of Homer is a standard. But he's more appreciated for his biting satire and keen intellect. At a time when Catholics were subject to absurdly oppressive penal laws—they couldn't even live within ten miles of London—Pope managed not only to survive but to convince the whole nation that he was England's greatest poet.

The Twentieth Century and Beyond

G.K. Chesterton was famous for his paradoxical way of putting things. Actually, he didn't think of his writing as paradoxical. In a world gone mad, sanity sounds like madness. Chesterton spent his life trying to hold fast to that which was good when the world around him wanted to toss centuries of wisdom and tradition in the rubbish bin.

Even though he lived only into middle age, Chesterton left an enormous pile of books behind him. The man seemed to be always writing—novels, essays, poems, detective stories, magazine articles. We could say that he wrote as he thought or that writing was his way of thinking. He looked back on history, and a pattern emerged. He wrote down what he saw, and eventually he wrote his way from agnosticism into the Catholic Church.

Orthodoxy—a book Chesterton wrote before he had made his final decision to enter the Catholic Church—is one of his most popular books among Catholics and one that very clearly expresses what makes him such a revelation for generation after generation. In it he describes his own journey from agnosticism to belief, which was prompted not by Christian apologists but by the detractors of Christianity, whose mutually contradictory accusations made Christianity seem strange and unique. It was too pessimistic, and it was too unrealistically joyful; it was too peaceful, and it was the source of all wars; it was too contemptuous of women, and only contemptible women believed in it. After a while it began to occur to Chesterton that perhaps the accusations were so contradictory because they came from one far side or the other, and Christianity was actually in the middle.

> Perhaps (in short) this extraordinary thing is really the ordinary thing; at least the normal thing, the center. Perhaps, after all, it is Christianity that is sane and all its critics that are mad—in various ways.[4]

Graham Greene, on the other hand, was a man who hated to be called a "Catholic writer." He was deeply Catholic in his faith, but he preferred to be judged by his writing, not by his religion.

Nevertheless, *The Power and the Glory,* probably his most famous novel, is about an explicitly Catholic subject: a worldly and sinful priest trying to survive in the state of Tabasco in Mexico, at a time when the fanatical Marxist government was trying to kill all priests.

It was a very personal story for Greene, because he had come to faith while living in Tabasco, where he had gone to avoid a prison sentence for libel. (He had written a scathing review of a Shirley Temple movie, and when the American studio decided to sue, England's notoriously plaintiff-friendly libel laws left him no alternative but flight.) In Tabasco, he was so moved by the unshakable faith of the poor, in spite of the best efforts of their supposed protectors in the government to extinguish it, that he felt there must be something to it.

Greene made a sharp distinction between his serious novels and his "entertainments," which were often spy stories. But even in his entertainments he couldn't help but deal with the same big questions that haunted his serious novels. Look at *The Third Man,* for example, which he wrote as a story to be made into a movie—widely considered one of the great masterpieces of the cinema. An American writer comes to bombed-out postwar Vienna only to find that the friend he has come to see is dead—or at least seems to be. As the story progresses, the American has to solve a strangely convoluted mystery in which nothing is what it seems to be.

But what really drives the plot is not the mystery but the moral decisions our hero has to make. Should he concentrate on winning the pretty girl he's fallen in love with, who seems to be up to her neck in whatever is going on? Does he owe his loyalty to his old friend? Or is there a higher moral law that he must obey, whatever the cost?

Big questions like those don't go away. Graham Greene, sinner that he was, spent his whole life searching for the answers to big questions. He was convinced that the Catholic Church was really the only place the answers could be found.

Today big questions still haunt new generations of writers. You may not know them as Catholic. They may not always even know themselves as Catholic. But when they confront the big questions we all have to face eventually, they're probably seeing them through a Catholic lens—if only because they've grown up reading the works of the great Catholic writers of the past and present.

CHAPTER SEVEN

Yours Is the Church That Made Women People

Every once in a while, we see something in the paper about a gruesome archaeological discovery—hundreds of infant skeletons found in a Roman-era ditch somewhere. Journalists write the story with breathless shock and horror, and the archaeologists play along because it's great publicity for their dig. But the archaeologists are never really surprised. They know exactly what they've dug up, and they know why it's there. It's another human garbage dump filled with unwanted babies. And as the archaeologists also know, it goes without saying that most of them are girls.

It was a simple economic fact of Roman life that a female child was worthless. Many of them were brought up anyway because their parents gave in to their natural affection. But many others were thrown away, either because their parents couldn't afford the cost of a girl or because they simply didn't want the trouble of raising one.

For pagan Romans, the female half of the species was always the property of the male. And she was the sort of property that was usually more liability than asset.

Why Girls Were Garbage

Like all children, male and female, a little girl was the property of her father. One could never expect her to make any contribution to the family's wealth, but she would cost a great deal just to feed. Then, when she reached marriageable age—about twelve years old, because there was no point in hanging on to her any longer than that—the family would have to find a husband to take her off their hands.

If the girl was very beautiful, her family might be lucky enough to find some besotted old fool who cared only for that. But generally they'd have to shell out a fat dowry to the man who finally took her. The expense might be ruinous, but the alternative was the expense of keeping her fed and clothed for the rest of her life, not to mention the shame of having a daughter no one would marry.

Once the girl was married, at least she was no trouble to her father anymore. Now she was the property of her husband, to be dealt with as he pleased.

Boys were different, of course. A boy had accomplishments to look forward to. He would carry on his father's legacy and bring honor to the family. He would be a useful citizen to the state, and perhaps he would even be called to some distinguished public service. A man was a person, and a woman was not.

A woman had no say in the affairs of the state—her testimony was not admissible evidence in court, for example. But legally women also had no say in the affairs of their own families. A woman had no legal or moral existence apart from the man who was responsible for her: her father if she was unmarried, her husband if she was married, and her son if she was a widow. If she was a widow and she had no son—well, she was nobody at all.

Fundamentally, a girl was useless because she would never be *someone*. She would never be distinguished or accomplished. She would never make her family proud of her. The best that could be hoped for was that she would eventually give birth to sons—sons for her husband's family, not for her father's.

Is it any wonder that, looking ahead to twelve or fifteen years of all loss and no profit, a father might rationally decide that there was no point in keeping a baby girl? The solution was simple. If a girl baby was born in the house, the family could just get rid of her. There was no need to kill her outright: One could just leave her out somewhere, and then her fate was in the gods' hands. Not that the gods usually intervened in these cases—but they could if they wanted to, couldn't they?

The Romans even had a technical term for this "final solution" to the girl problem. They called it *expositio*, or "exposure." Literally, the word *expositio* means "putting out," in the same way that we "put out" the garbage on trash night.

Neither Male nor Female

You can imagine what a shock it was to the Romans to hear those strange Christians proclaiming that in Christ "there is neither male nor female" (Galatians 3:28). But that was the Christian way.

When women spoke to him, Christ listened. If Christ himself paid attention to what the women around him had to say, no Christian could dismiss women as not worth listening to.

Does that mean Christian women lived in perfect equality with men? Did Christian men always treat women as intellectual equals? No, of course not. All are sinners; Christians often fail to live up to our most exalted principles. But Christians did treat women very differently from the way ordinary pagans treated them.

We have two proofs of that. One is the huge number of women who converted to Christianity, showing that they were definitely finding something they were looking for in the new faith. The other is the writings we have by the Christians themselves—some of them actually by women, which was almost unheard-of in those days, and some of them stories of great women and their heroic deeds, which was just as unheard-of.

The great epics of pagan culture were always stories of warriors—men who fought bravely and either died in battle or succeeded in taking possession of a kingdom. Either way, the hero always did a lot of killing of his rivals. In fact, we can confidently say that in all pagan literature, there's no such thing as an epic hero who never killed anyone.

Line after line of Homer is devoted to loving descriptions of eviscerations and dismemberments, all in colorful and intimate medical detail. Open the *Iliad* almost at random, and you'll find something like this:

...But Merion, as he fled,
Sent after him a brazen lance, that ran his eager head
Through his right hip, and all along the bladder's region
Beneath the bone; it settled him, and set his spirit gone
Amongst the hands of his best friends; and like a worm
  he lay
Stretch'd on the earth, which his black blood imbrued,
  and flow'd away.[1]

87

The clinical details of how the spear entered the body are a typical Homeric touch.

The Christians, on the other hand, had very different epic heroes: the martyrs, who showed that they were heroes by refusing to fight. They died without lifting a sword, let alone felling a hundred men in one charge. Bodily strength had nothing to do with this sort of heroism. Now a hero didn't have to be a young man in the prime of his manly vigor. It could be an old woman, or a new mother, or a twelve-year-old girl.

St. Agnes

St. Agnes of Rome was a twelve-year-old girl who had been promised in marriage to a much older man—which was quite common in those days. Her father probably congratulated himself on getting rid of an odious daughter so early. But Agnes insisted that she belonged to Christ and no other man. Her would-be husband turned her in to the government as a Christian, and she was hauled before the court.

One legend tells us that the judge, thinking he might teach her a good lesson about refusing men's demands, sent her to a brothel, where she was miraculously protected, the customers refusing to touch her. At last she was brought back and tortured some more, and then condemned to death. She went to her death happy in the knowledge that she would soon be with her true Bridegroom.

Soon after the death of St. Agnes, the persecutions ended. Constantine had come to the throne, and he had declared himself a Christian. Was it the heroic death of Agnes that had made the moment ripe for a Christian emperor? Had the cruel and bloodthirsty Romans, whose idea of a good show was to see captives tortured to death in the arena, finally been shamed to their souls by the courage of a twelve-year-old girl? We don't know. But we do know that the people of Rome told Agnes's story over and over again. She became their symbol of virtuous innocence winning the ultimate victory over cruel tyranny. Now the most popular hero in Roman story was not the warrior Aeneas but a young girl who calmly allowed her tormentors to kill her.

But what gave women, and even young girls, this courage that put pagan men to shame? And why did women flock to the new faith in such numbers?

Maybe it was because Christianity gave them something they could never have had before: the right to be themselves.

Christian Liberation

Today pop culture tends to emphasize what Christians give up, especially when it comes to sex. Wasn't pagan Rome a paradise of free and indiscriminate sex? And didn't the Christians just ruin it all when they came along?

There's actually a certain truth to that story. A man who had money and position could get whatever kind of sex he wanted. Of course, those men made up a tiny part of the population. For the rest, pagan Rome was more like a hell of indiscriminate sex. Slaves, who made up a large part of the population, could be raped with impunity. Girls were married off at the age of twelve. Boys just expected to have to submit to the lecherous attentions of adult men.

For these 99 percent, Christian morality came as an emancipation, not a restriction. They didn't have to put up with the sexual injustices of the nobility anymore. A woman didn't have to lie back and take it, even if she was a slave. She was the image of God. She had a right—in fact, a duty—to control her own body.

She was not defined by the men in her life: She could actually be herself. She even had the option of joining herself to Christ, forsaking all others.

Certainly one of the best indications of how far women had come in the new Christian world was the remarkable group of talented women who gathered around St. Jerome. The world had never seen anything like it. Pagan antiquity has passed down the names of two or three female philosophers in the course of about a thousand years of thought. But in Rome, and later at Bethlehem, was a whole school of brilliant intellectuals, all of them women. Men listened to what they had to say; they turned to them for guidance when faced with thorny questions of heresy and orthodoxy.

These women all lived in consecrated celibacy. Dedicating themselves to Christ alone, they no longer belonged to any other man. They weren't appendages: They were individuals, with minds of their own. And they earned for the rest of womankind the right to be taken seriously.

There was Marcella, for example—the one Jerome sometimes called a slave driver because she asked him questions that even he couldn't answer, costing him whole nights of research in his library. Jerome credits her as the one who showed the orthodox party how to deal with a sudden eruption of heresy in the city of Rome.

Some of the early Church fathers thought there could be no women teachers (based on 1 Corinthians 14:34–35; 1 Timothy 2:11–12). But that didn't end up being the doctrine of the Catholic Church at all. The Church has not only listened to women as teachers but has actually declared several of them doctors of the Church—teachers whose works have been exceptionally important for our understanding of Christian truth. (In Latin the word *doctor* means "teacher," as it still does in our university degrees, like "doctor of philosophy.")

St. Catherine of Siena

One of those great doctors of the Church was St. Catherine of Siena, who lived in the late 1300s. This was a time when, as it turned out, the pope himself needed a good talking-to from a woman who wouldn't take no for an answer.

St. Catherine was never healthy, and she lived only thirty-three years. But that was long enough to change history. (Jesus himself lived on earth only thirty-three years, and in that time he changed everything.)

Catherine had visions of Jesus when she was very young, and at the age of seven she vowed celibacy. When she was still a young girl, she decided that she wanted to join the Dominicans. At first her mother wasn't very happy with that decision, but when Catherine became even sicker, her mother decided that her vocation was probably for the best after all.

Catherine's real career as a history changer began when she started writing letters—or rather dictating them, although her biographers tell us she was perfectly capable of writing in both Italian and Latin. She started by writing letters to people she knew well and gradually expanded her correspondence to a wider circle. One of her frequent correspondents was the pope, Gregory IX.

The Church as an institution had fallen into a sorry state in Catherine's time. The papacy, after a peak of power in the 1200s, had become the toy of the French kings. The popes were now living in Avignon in southern France rather than in Rome, and when the Avignon popes intervened in temporal affairs, it was always on the side of France. Though they never taught heresy, their naked partisanship in politics badly damaged the reputation of the papacy and the whole Church hierarchy.

Catherine was convinced that the only way to cure this festering sore in the Church was to move the papacy back to Rome, where it belonged. She was eloquent and convincing when she visited Pope Gregory XI; thus she had her way. The following year Gregory moved his whole court back to Rome.

The Church and Women Today

What about today? Has the Church lost its way and fallen behind the times?

More likely the times have fallen behind the Church. Today the Church often seems to be the only thing standing up and speaking out against the rampant exploitation of women in modern culture. Once again we see women treated as objects, not people. They may have the same legal rights as men, but women are judged by their sexual desirability, not by their minds. As our culture grows more pornographic, the problem gets worse.

In the middle of this return to pagan morality, there is one voice crying in the wilderness, saying, "Women are people, not toys." That voice comes from the Catholic Church. She will always defend the rights of women and proclaim their dignity.

CHAPTER EIGHT

Yours Is the Church That Made Children People

"Let the children come to me," Jesus told his disciples (Matthew 19:14). He had to tell them that because the disciples were shooing the little ones away. Children should be seen and not heard—well, preferably not seen either.

Jesus had a different idea about children: "To such belongs the kingdom of heaven." It was almost as if he thought children were people too. The Teacher had a lot of strange ideas.

In chapter seven we talked about the status of children in pre-Christian times. The short version is that they had no status. Children were property, to be disposed of as their fathers wished. Under Roman law a father had the power of life and death over his children. That law was mitigated in late pagan times, after one or two very public cases—in which fathers killed their sons—had outraged even the pagan sensibilities of Rome.

But the law was only the extreme expression of what every good Roman regarded as the natural order of things. Children were not people. At best a (male) child was a potential person. He was somewhat valuable for what he might become in the future:

a useful citizen of the state and a man who would carry on his father's name and reputation.

For the Christians, on the other hand, a child was a person, even before birth. Jesus gave us his example: We are to welcome the little children and even try to imitate them in their simplicity. And we are to care for them as fellow images of God, not just from the moment they come into the world but from the moment they are conceived.

Abortion

We know that abortion was very common among pagan Romans. It was a terribly dangerous practice. Abortion is dangerous to the mother (never mind the child) even today, but in Roman times—when there were no X-rays, no anesthesia, no measures for preventing infection—the chance of death was very high. Even higher was the chance of a serious injury that might lead to permanent infertility.

Still, women had abortions because the alternative might look to them far worse. A woman who had been unfaithful to her husband or a girl who had disgraced her father's house might very well conclude that the danger of being murdered was much greater than the risks of an abortion.

But what awful risks they were! The famous physician Celsus gave revoltingly detailed instructions for performing abortions. He did warn that the surgeon had to be very careful, and even then the risks were high.[1]

The Christian writer Tertullian described the abortion kit that surgeons carried with them, and that description is enough to show us how dangerous the procedure must have been. Remember, as you read it, that the Romans had no notions of sterilization of medical equipment. Even hand washing (without soap, since there wasn't any) was a peculiar custom with which the Jews saddled themselves.

> ...[A]mong surgeons' tools there is a certain instrument, which is formed with a nicely-adjusted flexible frame for opening the *uterus* first of all, and keeping it open; it is further furnished with [a ring-shaped] blade, by means of which the limbs within the womb are dissected with anxious but unfaltering care; its last appendage being a blunted or covered hook, [with which] the entire *fetus* is extracted by a violent delivery. There is also...a copper needle or spike, by which the actual death is managed in this furtive robbery of life: they give it, from its infanticide function, the name of [the baby-killer]—[since they recognize that the infant] was of course alive.[2]

For Christians, abortion was a dreadful crime, no matter what the circumstances. Tertullian goes on to say,

> Indeed for us murder is forbidden once and for all, so it is not permitted even to destroy what is conceived in the womb. To prohibit the birth of a child is only a faster way to murder; it makes little difference whether one destroys a life already born or prevents it from coming to birth. It is a human being, who is to be a human being, for the whole fruit is already present in the seed.

Sometimes theologians argued about exactly when the soul entered the fetus, but the question hardly mattered to their opinion of abortion. St. Augustine is often brought up in the arguments for abortion, because he debated whether early abortions ought to be punished as severely as later ones. But we can't construe that he didn't condemn abortion unconditionally. To Augustine even birth control was practically equivalent to murder.

If the child was already uniquely valuable inside the womb, obviously it was not because of its accomplishments. It was because every child is a unique creation in the image of God. That alone was enough to give it the dignity of a human being.

Infanticide and Exposure

If Christians utterly prohibited abortion, they certainly wouldn't condone infanticide. Today it seems so obvious to us that infanticide is wrong that we have a hard time understanding just how radical the Christian position was. Christians were setting themselves directly against the ancient fundamental law of Rome, the Twelve Tables, passed down from the time of the half-mythological kings. A father was specifically granted the right to discard a newborn infant if it was a girl or if it was a boy but defective in some way. Infanticide was considered good social policy.

In fact, one of the basic laws of Rome was that children who were deformed in any way not only could but ought to be killed. The ancient republican laws of the *Decemviri* (the ten men who were appointed to write a sort of Roman constitution) specifically said so—and they were in line with the general tenor of pagan thought. The much-admired code of Lycurgus, the lawgiver of Sparta, made exactly the same demand. It was a waste of resources to raise children who could never be useful to the state.

> ...And, indeed, Lycurgus was of a persuasion that children were not so much the property of their parents as of the whole commonwealth....

Nor was it in the power of the father to dispose of the child as he thought fit; he was obliged to carry it before certain triers at a place called Lesche; these were some of the elders of the tribe to which the child belonged; their business it was carefully to view the infant, and, if they found it stout and well made, they gave order for its rearing, and allotted to it one of the nine thousand shares of land above mentioned for its maintenance, but, if they found it puny and ill-shaped, they ordered it to be taken to what was called the Apothetae, a sort of chasm under Taygetus; as thinking it neither for the good of the child itself, nor for the public interest, that it should be brought up, if it did not, from the very outset, appear made to be healthy and vigorous.

For the same reason, the women did not bathe the new-born children with water, as is the custom in all other countries, but with wine, to test the temper and complexion of their bodies; from a notion they had that epileptic and weakly children faint and waste away when they are thus bathed, while, on the contrary, those of a strong and vigorous habit acquire firmness and get a temper by it, like steel.[3]

This is the historian Plutarch writing admiringly of the ancient Spartan lawgiver at just about the same time John the evangelist was writing his Gospel. A child had no right to life simply because he or she existed: There was a test to pass the moment one came out of the womb, to earn the right to all the trouble and expense of bringing the child up.

Roman law or tradition also set aside specific places in the city where unwanted children could be left to die—or to be collected by someone who wanted them, though everyone knew that was unlikely. And it's hard to say whether the ones who were rescued were the lucky ones. By law they were slaves.

It might be useful to have child slaves for menial tasks that required small fingers, but it would be difficult to turn a profit if you had to spend several years feeding and caring for the child before he or she could do any useful work. The one business that was likely to be profitable enough to make the effort worthwhile was prostitution. Child prostitutes were a specialty that might bring in a good price. And since they were both children and slaves—objects, not people—it didn't matter how they were used, did it?

Taking Care of Foundlings

Things started to change when the Christians gained the upper hand in the empire. They did not succeed in eradicating poverty and slavery, but they did change the assumptions about the nature of a slave and the nature of a child. Christians rescued children left out to die. Then the Christian emperor Gratian made infanticide a crime of murder. By the time of Justinian, foundlings were no longer slaves.

It's worth remembering just how countercultural this Christian idea was. Children are people? They have a right to life?

After a while it became common for churches to have a marble box or basin at the entrance where children could be left by parents who, for whatever reason, weren't able to take care of them. These rescued children became the responsibility of the Church, and when there were enough of them, special arrangements had to be made for their care. It is a remarkable fact that the darkest years of the Dark Ages—the 600s and 700s—are also the time when we see the first foundling asylums popping up in Europe. In the chaos of constant war and decline, the Church nevertheless found resources for what was really important—making sure that the children nobody wanted were taken care of.

Throughout the Middle Ages the Church continued to make sure that there were orphanages and foundling asylums available for the most helpless of God's children. Even today, in your own city, you'll probably find that the largest adoption agency is a Catholic institution.

The Horror of Sexual Abuse

It's a bit ironic that the most frequent insults hurled at Catholics these days have to do with the sex-abuse scandals of the last few years. It is indeed a horrible thing that there were priests who abused their unique positions of trust, and we should be ashamed of and pray for forgiveness for each case we didn't recognize soon enough to prevent damage. It's also true that Catholic priests are no more likely to be abusers than other people who have contact with youth. Sexual abuse by priests is a rare thing in any case, but it stands out because of the horror that sexually abusing a child inspires in us.

But where does that horror come from? Certainly the pagan Romans wouldn't have shared it. On the contrary, it was considered quite ordinary that a Roman aristocrat should have a good-looking boy to share his bed. And child prostitution, as we've already seen, was no big deal.

No, our righteous indignation at the sexual abuse of children doesn't come from ancient Roman ideals. Nor does it come from the Greeks, who gave us much of their philosophy and political thought. Pederasty was the norm, not the exception, for an Athenian intellectual at the time of Socrates. That was what happened to boys and young men; then they grew up to be men and found boys of their own.

Socrates himself was quite smitten with the young Alcibiades, who grew up to be one of the dictators of Athens—with no damage to his reputation from having been the lover of Socrates. If anything, people thought Socrates brought out Alcibiades's good side, and that if Alcibiades had spent more time in his bed, he might have turned out better.

So our natural horror at child abuse—which by the way, is a good sign that our culture, for all its faults, may still be reasonably healthy—didn't come from the Greeks or the Romans. It came from the Christians. It was the Church that taught us to acknowledge the sacred rights of children as human beings.

The world judges Catholics by Christian standards now; the Christian victory has been so complete that it's practically invisible. When the babbling bloggers blame us for being Christians, they're really blaming us for not being Christian enough. Christian principles seem like part of the order of nature, laws as immutable as gravity and magnetism. But that's only because the Church succeeded, against all odds, in replacing what everyone thought was an immutable law of nature with a strange Christian idea—such as the notion that children are people too.

Yours is the Church that conquered the world with the meekness of a child.

CHAPTER NINE

Yours Is the Church of Human Dignity

As far as Christians are concerned, all human beings are equally important, because all human beings are *infinitely* important. We are all brothers and sisters because God is our Father. And Christ came to save us all.

Science tells us these days that all human beings have a common origin and that all human races are equal. Christians have always known that, but scientists haven't. Many thinkers of the past, people who considered themselves entirely rational, argued that the different human races must have had different origins. Even the ones who accepted a common origin were mostly convinced that some races were by nature superior to others.

European scientists naturally found evidence that Europeans were superior to other races and that the natives of their own country were superior to other Europeans. The inferiority of certain races was an accepted "scientific" fact. If you look up *Negro* in the 1911 *Encyclopedia Britannica*, there it is in black and white, so to speak:

In certain of the characteristics mentioned above the negro would appear to stand on a lower evolutionary plane than the white man, and to be more closely related to the highest anthropoids....

Mentally the negro is inferior to the white.... But though the mental inferiority of the negro to the white or yellow races is a fact, it has often been exaggerated....[1]

Against such scientific certainty, the Church's teaching must have seemed quaint if not ludicrous. "There is neither Jew nor Greek, there is neither slave nor free, there is neither male nor female; for you are all one in Christ Jesus" (Galatians 3:28). And just to make sure we don't think one race or another is somehow excluded, Scripture takes some trouble to point out that one of the earliest Christian converts was Ethiopian (see Acts 8:26–39).

Slavery

In the pagan world, slaves were property. And you could do anything you liked with your property. A master could rape his female slaves—or for that matter, his male ones—as much as he liked. Who would dare tell him he couldn't do what he liked with what belonged to him?

The Christians would.

Christians didn't eliminate slavery, and maybe we should be ashamed that we didn't. But they did draw a very clear line. Slave or not, they said, a person's a person. In Christ there is neither slave nor free. So, for example, one of the most breathtakingly revolutionary laws of the Christian emperors made it illegal to rape a slave. If a slave woman was raped by her master, she was automatically set free, out of the power of her rapist.

The law was revolutionary because it moved slaves from the category of things to the category of people. But if slaves were property, didn't they cease to be persons? No, said the Christians—and when they had the power, they gave their principles the force of law. The dignity of personhood belongs to us because we are all created in the image of God. It doesn't go away if we happen to be slaves. A slave may be bound to service, but she can't be bound to give up her virtue. This was a protective wall the Christians built around human dignity.

Bartholomé de las Casas

Bartholomé de las Casas, a Spaniard, was probably about eight years old when Columbus made his famous voyage in 1492. Two years later he moved with his father to the new Spanish colony on Hispaniola, the island now divided between Haiti and the Dominican Republic.

The Spanish colonists there had set up a brutal system of exploiting the native population. They enslaved the ones they thought might be useful. Bartholomé and his father owned some of these native slaves, and they participated in slave-hunting expeditions to capture more of them. These expeditions were necessary because many of the Spanish landowners were so unrelentingly cruel, and worked their slaves so incessantly, that they were quickly worn out. There were always dead slaves to be replaced.

Bartholomé had always been attracted to the priesthood, and in 1510 he became the first Catholic priest ordained in the New World. In that same year a group of Dominican friars came to Hispaniola. They were so appalled by the cruelty they saw there that they refused confession to the slave owners—including Bartholomé.

These Dominicans were naturally unpopular among the Spanish landowners, who managed to have them sent back to Europe— but not before one of them preached a fire-and-brimstone sermon that made a lasting impression on Bartholomé. The Dominican told the colonists that every slave who fell dead from overwork had been murdered. No law could justify the Spaniards' incessant wars against the inoffensive natives.

Bartholomé had joined the other landowners in their protest against the Dominicans. But that sermon! He couldn't get it out of his head.

Three years later, Bartholomé went as a chaplain with an expedition to Cuba. The soldiers had been wreaking their usual havoc there, but Bartholomé was able to build such a good rapport with the peaceful Cuban natives that they would do anything he asked them to do. He used his influence with them to make sure the Spanish had no cause for hostility as they wandered through the island. Wherever the soldiers went, the natives would bring them gifts of food and set aside a place for them to stay in their towns.

But this wasn't enough to keep the ignorant and bloodthirsty soldiers in check. One day—no one really knows why—the soldiers went berserk and started hacking down a crowd of unarmed Cubans in the middle of their village. Bartholomé heard the screams of the dying and quickly ran to the scene, where he found that half the village had already been slaughtered. The commander, Panfilo de Narvaez, was just looking on. He hadn't lifted a finger to stop the massacre.

With cool indifference Narvaez asked Bartholomé, "What do you think of what our Spaniards have done?"

"To hell with you and your Spaniards!" Bartholomé spat back furiously.

With much shouting and quite a bit of language more typical of a soldier than of a priest, Bartholomé finally put a stop to the slaughter. Then he could do nothing but give baptism to the dying. It was a moment he could never forget—the horror was seared into his memory.

It was the year after that, 1514, that Bartholomé made his final break with the Spanish establishment. He was scheduled to preach at Mass on Pentecost, so he looked for a suitable text. And he found it in the book of Sirach:

> To take away a neighbor's living is to murder him;
>   to deprive an employee of his wages is to shed blood.
> (Sirach 34:22)

These words opened his eyes to the fact that the whole Spanish system was rotten, sinful, and murderous. And the murderers were not just the soldiers who drew the sword. Anyone who held native slaves was a murderer, because the slaves were dying from their servitude. And Bartholomé owned slaves! He was as guilty as the rest of them!

Bartholomé knew that he could not push for justice while he kept slaves. He went straight to the Spanish governor of the colony and told him that he was turning over his slaves to the governor's protection. He said that he would spend the rest of his life trying to make the Spanish see the monstrous injustice of what they were doing.

The governor was a good friend of his, but he thought Bartholomé had lost his mind. He tried to persuade Bartholomé not to throw away so much valuable human property. But there was no reasoning with the crazy priest. He had made his decision, and he was going to stick with it.

But what could one priest do? It was perfectly obvious that the colonial landowners weren't going to listen to him. No, there was only one way to bring real reform, and that was by going over their heads—not to the governor but to the king of Spain himself.

Bartholomé spent most of the rest of his life trying to bring justice to the natives of the New World. He made trips to Europe and back—at a time when a voyage across the Atlantic was the ultimate adventure. He lobbied princes and popes. He tried to set up utopian communities where the natives could live unmolested, but his attempts were foiled by slave traders.

Bartholomé made himself so unpopular in the colonies that he repeatedly had to flee for his life. Sometimes it seemed as though he could make no headway against the powerful landowners, who had no desire to lose their slaves. Even after he was made bishop of Chiapas in Mexico, he found that he didn't really have the power to stop the colonists' abuses.

But Bartholomé never gave up. He held to the principle that all human beings were equally children of God, that a Spaniard was in no way naturally better than a Cuban. In fact, a Spaniard's mistreatment of the natives made him a great deal worse.

His opponents were prepared to argue that the Indians were not really human at all, and in that argument they had the support of much of the "enlightened scientific opinion" of the day. Bartholomé, on the other hand, had Scripture. And he had such a hair-raising story of massacres and atrocities that he was able to gain the rhetorical upper hand.

At last he won something of a victory from the Spanish government. New laws made the natives subjects of the crown. They were no longer the property of the individual landowners; theoretically they were equal citizens.

It was, in some ways, a hollow victory, because the colonists simply refused to abide by the new laws. And most of the natives of Hispaniola and Cuba were already dead, whole populations eradicated in one generation. But it did establish the principle in the secular government that there is only one human race, not a master race and a subject race.

By far the greater victory, however, was in the Church. Bartholomé reaffirmed what Christians have known since St. Paul wrote it: As far as Christ is concerned, there are no differences between races or nations—there are only children of God. He held his own against the "enlightened" thinkers who insisted that there was no point in treating the American natives as people.

And the Church came down on Bartholomé's side. While adventurers were trying to squeeze gold out of the American natives, the priests who followed them stood up for human dignity, sometimes actually putting themselves between the oppressors and the oppressed. Yours is the Church that demanded equality for all races when the very idea seemed absurd to educated Europeans.

The faith of millions in Latin America today is a testament to the depth of Bartholomé's victory. In the dark days of slavery and oppression, millions of Americans turned to the Church as their protector. They knew that the faith of people like Bartholomé and the brave priests who followed him could not be empty. They embraced it as their own and became truly faithful Catholics, even while the dissolute colonists were mostly worshiping mammon.[2]

Secular Fanatics

We've seen how the Church has fought for equality and dignity in the past. But what about the present?

We live at a moment in history when religious fanaticism looks like the great enemy of freedom. With zealots blowing up crowded markets and beheading teenage girls, we can certainly see that fanaticism is an evil and dangerous thing. But the fashionable atheists would argue that religion itself is the problem—that atheists would never be so brutal and persecuting. They can make that argument only because they've forgotten what the world was like thirty years ago.

For two hundred years, from the French Revolution to the fall of the Soviet Union, the main enemy of peace and freedom was dogmatic atheism. The twentieth century was one long struggle for freedom against atheist zealots.

At the beginning of the twentieth century, the great fear of every peaceful citizen was the assorted anarchists and communists and their "dynamite outrages"—blowing up crowded markets, in other words. The face of terrorism was not the religious fanatic but the implacable rebel with a theory that had no room for religion.

Then came the Bolshevik Revolution in Russia, and suddenly those mad rebels were in charge of the largest country on earth. Almost immediately they set about extinguishing religion in Russia while simultaneously exporting their revolution to their neighbors in a series of bloody wars.

Meanwhile, in Germany, the Nazis took advantage of economic chaos and malingering ethnic hatred—not to mention fear of Russian-style communists—to worm their way into power and begin a campaign of oppression so brutal that the whole world uses *Nazi* as a synonym for "evil oppressor."

Hitler and his minions were smart enough to portray themselves as the champions of old-fashioned Christian morality. But of course they were nothing of the sort. Hitler himself was under no illusions about Christianity: "It's the same old Jewish swindle," he said.[3] After he took care of "the Jewish problem," the Catholic problem was next on his agenda.

As for the Protestants, the cooperative ones were easy to deal with: They accepted the Nazified version of Christianity, with the Old Testament cut out to purify the faith of its unsavory Jewish associations. The other ones ended up in concentration camps with the rest of the misfits.

The Nazi leaders themselves had nothing to do with Christianity. Some were simple atheists. Others—and a surprising number of these were the top leaders of the movement—had occult ideas that we can only call wacky. SS head Heinrich Himmler, for example, spent a fortune on setting up a castle modeled on King Arthur's mythical Camelot. He hired a pet archaeologist to find the actual Holy Grail. (The archaeologist failed, and mysteriously fell off a mountain shortly afterward.)

The core idea of Nazi thought was extreme nationalism. The German nation, or rather those parts of it that were "ethnically pure" (whatever that meant), was the master race. It had to defeat all inferior nations in a Darwinian battle for ethnic survival. The more intelligent classes among those inferior nations would be destroyed; the rest would be enslaved and probably allowed to die naturally from the effects of hard labor and malnutrition.

Meanwhile, the Soviet leadership had passed to Josef Stalin, who was perhaps more pragmatic than Hitler but just as good at eliminating large populations. In the officially atheist Soviet Union, the one thing you couldn't be was religious. It's almost miraculous that a stubby remnant of the Russian Orthodox Church was actually allowed to survive. In 1918, just after the Communist Revolution, there were about fifty thousand Orthodox priests in Russia; by 1935, only seventeen years later, there were about five hundred. Out of every hundred priests, ninety-nine had vanished—many of them sent to prison or executed.

After the Second World War, the Soviet Union took over most of Eastern Europe, installing puppet governments in Poland, East Germany, Hungary, Czechoslovakia, Romania, and Bulgaria and annexing much of the territory it hadn't previously. Atheism was made the official policy in all those countries, and religion was persecuted in various mild to harsh ways.

Atheist ideologies took over many other parts of the world as well. China turned communist in 1949, and the Catholic Church is still an illegal underground organization in the most populous country in the world. Communist dictatorships rose up in Southeast Asia, in Africa, and in Central America; wherever they rose, religion was persecuted as the enemy of the people. Meanwhile, the 1970s were a kind of golden age of terrorism in the West, when fanatical left-wing groups of all sorts, but uniformly antireligious, blew people up at an alarming rate.

So the world was divided into two camps from about 1945 to 1990. A huge part of the earth's surface was controlled by officially atheist governments. Atheist fanatics sent people to reeducation camps or firing squads for the crime of being religious.

The other half of the world sometimes seemed scarcely better: In many countries brutal right-wing dictators took advantage of the popular fear of communism to install regimes that were every bit as oppressive as the communists they kept at bay.

Clearly fanatical atheism is just as persecuting as fanatical religion. And it has been far more efficient at killing.

This long excursion through the ugly parts of recent history has been necessary only because there are people today who seriously assert that religion naturally persecutes its opponents and that atheists never persecuted anybody. It's hard to tell whether such people suffer from extraordinary ignorance or from simple chutzpah.

The Polish Pope

The balance of power was suddenly unbalanced in 1978 when a cardinal from Poland, one of the officially atheist countries of Eastern Europe, was chosen as Pope John Paul II.

Poland had never been very successful at uprooting the Church. The communist authorities uneasily tolerated the Catholic hierarchy there. The Church continued to function, constantly bumping up against the restrictive government.

Nobody expected a Polish pope. There hadn't been a pope from outside Italy in four and a half centuries. A pope from the Soviet bloc—well, that changed everything. The people of Poland were stunned and—something they hadn't been in a long time—hopeful.

When Pope John Paul II visited Warsaw the year after his election, he had a simple message for the Polish people: "Do not be afraid." They had been afraid all their lives. Older people remembered the horrors of the Nazi occupation, and before that the horror of wondering whether their country would fall victim to

Hitler or Stalin first or—as it actually happened—both at the same time. And now the communist secret police were everywhere.

But here was a Polish pope—a man who had fearlessly resisted the Nazi occupation as part of the underground and then stood up to the communists. Maybe he was right. Maybe they didn't have to be afraid.

We know now from John Paul's own correspondence that even he didn't think communism could be uprooted in his lifetime. But he had faith that, whatever happened, good must ultimately prevail. It was the same faith that had carried him through the darkest days of the Nazi occupation, when life must have seemed hopeless to the people around him.

The year after John Paul's visit, the government—by now practically bankrupted by its own failed economic policies—announced a series of unpopular price increases. At once there was a huge wave of strikes all across the country. The Polish people had taken courage—and the Polish government didn't know what to do about it. Repressing such massive protests would require massacres on an enormous scale, and there was no guarantee that the government would win an open civil war. Eventually the communists caved in and allowed the formation of an independent trade union, Solidarity.

The union gave the resistance to communism a sharp focus. In spite of the government's attempts to suppress the movement, it kept pushing. In 1989 the communists finally bowed to the inevitable and allowed the first noncommunist government in Eastern Europe to form.

The shock wave rolled through the rest of the Soviet bloc with astonishing rapidity. One by one the other communist governments of Eastern Europe fell to massive protests. Finally, even the Soviet Union fell.

What had made everything happen so fast? The leaders on both sides had no doubt. It was the Polish pope, John Paul II, who had inspired the people of Eastern Europe to stand up for themselves. There were other forces at work—communism was burning itself out with economic failures—but it was the electrifying leadership of the pope who said, "Do not be afraid," that brought the people to their feet.

Yours is the Church that stood up to international communism, a worldwide despotism, and stared it down.

CHAPTER TEN

Yours Is the Church of World Peace

For most of the world, most of the time, the idea of world peace has been nonsense. War has been what men do to prove they are men; "virtue," the quality that makes men good fighters.

Then what could one make of this strange Christian idea that the "meek" would inherit the earth? We know who the meek are: They are the cowards who prefer peace to war. They don't inherit anything, and if they do, somebody who's strong and warlike takes it away from them.

Yet Christians dared to tell a world whose heroes were its most efficient killers that war was a bad thing. Christians told stories of their own heroes, men and women who had let themselves be killed rather than fight. For a Christian, dying without fighting could actually be better than fighting and winning! That made no sense at all.

And then there was the Christian idea of brotherhood. "Love your neighbor as yourself," the Christians said. And Christ had made it clear that by "neighbor" we were supposed to understand absolutely anyone in the whole world, even the foreigner who wasn't at all like us (see Luke 10:25–37).

A Just War?

Various philosophers in the ancient world grappled with the question of when war was justified, but all their contradictory speculations had little to do with the real world. At any rate they were all forgotten, along with literate culture in general, in the terrible wave after wave of invasions that the Roman world suffered in the 400s and 500s.

When the Goths or the Huns invaded the Roman Empire, they weren't doing it because the empire had oppressed them. They were doing it because war was their business. The nation was an army, to be led to war against somebody who had riches worth plundering. There were nations whose only source of prosperity lay in spoiling less warlike peoples of their treasures and their populations.

Against that barbarian ethic—and remember that those barbarians were the founders of modern Europe—the Catholic Church stood firm. War is always an evil, and in order for it to be justified, the effects of not going to war must be even worse.

Our old friend St. Thomas Aquinas (building on the ideas of St. Augustine) worked out the principles of just-war theory, and they've been refined over the centuries. The resulting guidelines are very restrictive. In Catholic doctrine there are four criteria that must *all* be met before it is legitimate to go to war against an aggressor:

— the damage inflicted by the aggressor on the nation or community of nations must be lasting, grave, and certain;

— all other means of putting an end to it must have been shown to be impractical or ineffective;

— there must be serious prospects of success;

— the use of arms must not produce evils and disorders graver than the evil to be eliminated. The power of modern means of destruction weighs very heavily in evaluating this condition. (CCC, 2309)

Catholics still argue about the idea of a "just war" and, in particular, about whether this or that conflict can be called "just." But the simple fact is that there is a standard, and everyone agrees that there is one. The world is so convinced of it that the most aggressive nations find they need to fabricate reasons for their aggression.

We've seen in modern times what happens when that broad consensus is set aside. Fascism dismissed the idea of justice and fell back on the old barbarian ethic. Nations are locked in a struggle for existence, the Nazis said in Germany and the Fascists said in Italy. The superior must make room for their expanding populations, and must gain the resources they need to grow, by conquering and eliminating the inferior. There was no need for an elaborate theory to justify aggression; aggression was simply what nations did to survive.

When the Nazis invaded Poland, the trumped-up pretext—a few border incidents staged by Nazis dressed as Poles—was so ridiculously transparent that no one took it seriously. "It doesn't matter whether it's plausible," Hitler had told his generals. "No one will ask the winner whether he told the truth."[1]

That even Hitler found it necessary to trump up some reason for his invasion shows how thoroughly the Christian idea of a just war had infected Western culture. And we can see the consequences of rejecting that idea. Hitler's invasion of Poland began the Second World War, by far the most destructive conflict in the history of the world. All the religious wars in history don't add up to the horror of those six years from 1939 to 1945.

War still goes on today, and we must admit that few of the wars today are in any way justified. But the Catholic idea of justice even in war is an extraordinarily powerful one. It holds back even the most aggressive leaders. For they know that some show of justice is essential for their standing among the nations and that some show of proportionality in fighting is the only thing that will keep them from being locked out of the world community.

The Crusades

In spite of all the deep thought that went into the doctrine of a just war, it's clear that Catholics have sometimes applied these doctrines in ways that are hard to justify. Usually they started out with good intentions, and then things spiraled out of control before the leaders of the Church could do anything to stop them. The Crusades are a good example.

There was a good reason for crusading at the beginning. The brutal repression of Christians in the Holy Land had shocked the Christian world. Dangerous new invaders threatened the very existence of Christendom.

Palestine had been in Muslim hands for centuries, but for most of that time the repression was a dull ache rather than a sharp pain. Christians had to show every day that they were second-class citizens, and the laws that barely tolerated their religion were designed to make sure that Christianity slowly faded away.

Christians couldn't have crosses on their churches or sound bells that Muslims could hear. They couldn't pray too loudly. They couldn't ride horses, because that might make them taller than a passing Muslim. Often they had to wear distinctive clothing or put signs on their houses so that Muslims would know they were the wrong kind of people. They couldn't prevent their children from converting to Islam, and they couldn't try to persuade a Muslim to convert to Christianity. Muslim men could marry Christian women, but Christian men could not marry Muslim women.

Still, with all the restrictions, life was possible. Christian communities were still large, though shrinking slowly. Christian pilgrims from Europe regularly made journeys to the Holy Land, and in general they and their money were welcomed. In a world where the idea of "freedom of religion" didn't really exist, the situation was probably the best that could be hoped for. After all, life wasn't particularly easy for Muslims in Christian countries either.

Things changed when a new and bigoted ruler came to power. The "mad caliph" Hakim (as Christian historians remember him) burned the Church of the Holy Sepulcher and made life for Christians in the Holy Land not merely unpleasant but potentially deadly. A Turkish invasion made things even worse, threatening not only the Christians of the Holy Land but also the Roman Empire of the East, which was all that stood between Western Christendom and the expansion of the Islamic empire. Pilgrims could no longer safely travel to the Holy Land, because the Turks and the caliphate were at war.

All these things filled Western Europe with outrage and dread. When the emperor in Constantinople appealed for help, the First Crusade was launched as a kind of holy rescue mission.

It would be hard to justify the course some of the Crusades took after that. The Fourth Crusade, for example, gathered at Constantinople, the greatest city in the Christian world. The leaders of the Crusade decided that there was more booty to be had in that city than in Palestine. Whatever provocations they may have suffered from the Byzantines, the Crusaders couldn't have been in the right to sack and pillage a Christian city, destroying a thousand years of culture.

Religious wars and the Inquisition are sins against peace that people often bring up, and with some justice. Of course, the Church is full of sinners, and sometimes those sinners have sinned in the same way as the secular rulers of the time. It would be surprising if they hadn't. Certainly it's not good to say "He started it" and expect that to justify years of bloodshed.

It's true that the so-called "religious" wars in Europe were mostly started by one ruler or another who used religion as a pretext for his own selfish ends. But the Church could have been firmer and denounced the wars unambiguously.

The Inquisition

Probably the most notorious of the bad things that have happened in the Church is the Inquisition. It's also one of the least understood.

It's fair to say that most people today don't have a very good idea of what the Inquisition was. Our notions of it come from B movies and Monty Python sketches. Like every other long-term historical phenomenon, the Inquisition was complicated, and it changed over time and in different places.

In the beginning the Inquisition was meant to be an investigation. Its purpose was to find out who had been saying what and which things that had been said were not true. That had become important because of the rise of the Albigensian heresy, named for the town of Albi in southern France. The Albigensians believed a number of rather odd things, some of which you might argue were rather dangerous. Encouraged by sympathetic nobles (whose sympathy might have had more to do with secular politics than with religious conviction), Albigensian ideas spread over a large part of France, in some places almost completely displacing the orthodox Catholic Church.

What were the dangerous things about this heresy? And who had been teaching them? Which teachers should people believe? The first Inquisition was set up to answer these important questions.

There was no hard and fast separation between church and state in those days. The Church had its sphere, and the state had its sphere. But the Church was expected to tell the state what was correct in matters of religion, and the state used its power to make sure that its subjects stayed in the path of Catholic truth. To say that each person should decide which religion to follow probably would have sounded as absurd as to say that each person should decide which government to pay taxes to.

Inevitably, the Inquisition and the governments cooperated. The state rounded up suspected heretics to be examined. The Inquisition handed over convicted heretics to be punished by the state.

It didn't take long for secular powers to realize that the Inquisition could be managed as yet another weapon to wield against their enemies. In some of the most notorious Inquisitions—the Spanish Inquisition especially—the whole operation became an arm of the state, almost completely out of the control of Rome. It became a kind of war against the state's enemies rather than an inquiry into the truth of certain teachings.

So there are two things we have to remember about the Inquisition: First, it happened at a time when the notion of freedom of religion really didn't exist; and second, the secular governments actually perpetrated many of the evils we associate with the Inquisition.

That does not excuse the worst excesses. When cardinals, bishops, and priests sent people to be tortured for their beliefs, they were not acting the way Christ taught us to act. The teachings of Christ were available to them; they couldn't say that nobody had told them such violence was wrong.

Remembering the wicked things that were done in the name of Christ should make us all the more determined to stand up for freedom and against religious wars today. In much of the world, Catholic Christians are liable to the same sort of persecution that was inflicted on suspected heretics in the Middle Ages. It's easy for us to see how wrong it is when it's happening to us. What we need—and what the leaders of the Church have had—is the courage to admit where we were wrong and even to use our own failings as examples to the rest of the world of what happens when we let our prejudice overwhelm our love for our neighbors.

It's also wrong to dwell on these sins of Catholic Christians as if they were somehow characteristic of Catholic thought. In fact, the Catholic Church has been the world's most consistent advocate of peace for two millennia now. Let's look at the meeting between the world's most feared barbarian and the representative of world Christianity—and how the result of that meeting turned the world on its head.

Leo the Great and Attila the Scourge

In the 400s the Roman Empire suffered one catastrophic invasion after another. Vandals poured across the West and into Africa, leaving such a trail of devastation that we still call any act of wanton destruction "vandalism." Goths sacked the city of Rome itself; the "mistress of the world," which had not seen a foreign invader in eight centuries, was opened up to pillage by Germanic barbarians. Burgundians and Franks spilled into the peaceful and prosperous province of Gaul and made themselves at home. We still call the place France after the Franks, and the region where the Burgundians moved in is still called Burgundy.

But there was one invader so inhumanly destructive, so apparently unstoppable, that later historians called him the Scourge of God. His name was Attila, and his fierce Huns surged in from the East like a tsunami and destroyed everything in their path. One city after another fell amid horrible massacres; then Attila would extort some enormous tribute for a while, until he found the next excuse to go on a spree again. On the soldiers marched, defeating the weary and demoralized Romans in one battle after another, until it seemed as though God had ordained Attila for the destruction of the Roman Empire.

At last Attila entered Italy, still destroying cities as he went, until the city of Rome itself was within his grasp. Clearly nothing could save the city; every legion had been defeated, and the citizens were too worn out from all the previous disasters to offer any resistance, even if they had been able to match the numbers of Attila's horde. They had heard of what had happened to the people in the other cities Attila had taken. The city of Aquileia, once one of the fairest in the empire, had been simply wiped off the map. Now it looked like their turn to die. Who could save them?

Attila was conferring with his generals in his tent when a herald brought the announcement that a Roman ambassador had come to see him. This was news. Who had come to represent Rome before the mighty Attila? It had better be somebody important. Attila had already warned that he would accept no one below consular rank as an ambassador, and the Romans had learned from terrible experience that he was not willing to be flexible on that demand.

But it was not a consul or an ex-consul who had come to see the great conqueror. It was Leo, the pope. With no armed escort, no way of protecting himself if things went sour, Leo came to see the most dangerous man in the world—a pagan barbarian who worshiped strange and bloodthirsty gods—and ask him not to devastate Rome.

What did Leo say to Attila? We don't really know. We only know that he walked out of the terrible Hun's tent with the news that Rome was saved. Attila had agreed to retreat beyond the borders of the empire and live at peace with Rome. He did set some conditions, of course, leaving himself a loophole for a future invasion. But he proved a man of his word: He picked up his whole host and left Italy and the incalculable riches of Rome behind. (By the next year Attila was dead, so there was no future invasion.)

The people of Rome could hardly believe the news when they heard it. It must have been a miracle; there could be no other explanation. Modern historians are almost as baffled. Some offer halfhearted attempts at strategic considerations that might have turned Attila back. But Attila was never one to shy away from a battle, especially one he had a near certainty of winning.

If we discount a miracle, we're left with psychological explanations. Attila was very superstitious—a common fault among Romans of the era as well as their barbarian neighbors. He knew that the papacy was venerated throughout the Christian world and that—at least until Attila came—the Christian world had been incomparably more civilized and powerful than any other civilization he knew of. Perhaps he feared the wrath of the Christian God.

Pagans were very inclusive. Attila had his own gods, but he was open to the idea that other nations had theirs. Maybe this God of the Romans had some tricks up his sleeve that he hadn't shown yet. If Leo had enough confidence in his God to come out alone to meet Attila, perhaps he had some reason for that confidence.

Or perhaps the explanation is even simpler. Perhaps Attila the man was simply impressed by the courage of an unarmed bishop who would come to see him, the most dreaded man in the world, without showing any signs of fear.

Whatever it was, the Christian way confronted the barbarian way in that fateful meeting. And against all odds, the Christian way won.

Pope Leo the Great went on to be remembered as one of the greatest leaders Christianity has ever had. Attila's empire died with him. The nineteenth-century historian Thomas Hodgkin summed it up neatly: "The barbarian king had all material power in his hand, and he was working but for a twelvemonth. The Pontiff had no power but in the world of intellect, and his fabric was to last fourteen centuries."

CHAPTER ELEVEN

Yours Is the Church of the Future

Does the Catholic Church have a future?

You've probably seen that question asked in a dozen magazine or newspaper articles this year alone. Attendance is declining. The Church is rocked by scandal. Priests are laughingstocks in popular entertainment. Some governments seem to be actively hostile. How can the Church survive another generation?

All these things seem like very big problems. And they are. We shouldn't ignore them. But they're problems of the Church in one small corner of the world: the English-speaking countries and Western Europe. It's hard for us to think of ourselves as a small part of the world, but the world is a great deal bigger than our little slice of it.

The fact is that the Church as a whole is not contracting but expanding. More than a billion people all over the world are Catholics, and there are more of us every day. Many of the new converts are in Africa and Asia, the world's two largest and most populous continents. They live in places that our newspapers and magazines tend to ignore. But they're important members of the

Church of the future. With the continual expansion of travel and communication systems, chances are good that you and I will get to know some of them.

Can the Church and Science Work Together?

One of the problems pop culture has with the Church is that people tend to confuse science with ethics. Science is very good at telling us what is. In fact, that's a good definition of science: It's the method we use for discovering the truth about what *is*. But science can't tell us anything about what *ought to be*. That's where religion and ethics come in.

Now, many people who call themselves scientists would disagree with that last statement. But that's where they get into trouble. Science can tell us that certain actions have certain consequences. If you shoot a man in the head, he is very likely to die. But would that be a bad thing? Science can't say.

Perhaps science can look at statistics and show that, if people were allowed to go around shooting other people all the time, the human race would soon be extinct. But would that be a bad thing? Science can't say. We can say that we really don't want the human race to be extinct, but then we're not making a scientific statement.

Science may be able to measure our neural activity and tell us that we really do have a sincere desire for the race to continue, but science can't tell us whether that sincere desire is better or more important than the very sincere desire of the child who says, "But I don't *want* to go to bed!"

So when scientists tell us what ought to be, we need to remember that they're not speaking as scientists anymore. They may be speaking as very well-informed citizens: For example, they may be able to tell us that we could save a hundred thousand lives a year by taking a certain chemical off the market. But as soon as they say, "Therefore, it must be taken off the market," they're speaking ethically, not scientifically. That doesn't mean they're not right, but it does mean the statement isn't a scientific one.

All this is important because our pop culture seems to have the idea that religion can be replaced by science, now that we have so much knowledge about how the world works. And there are always people with agendas who would love to make us believe that their pronouncements are scientific truth.

So when we hear somebody saying that we now know the scientific truth about birth control, and therefore the Church must give up its opposition—or that we know the truth about abortion, so we must make sure it's legal—we have to remember that we're not hearing scientific statements. The Church isn't opposing science if it opposes abortion. It may be opposing certain scientists with opinions, but their opinions on ethical issues may not be worth any more than yours are. And it's certain that they're worth a great deal less than the teachings of the Church.

We can dismiss the idea that science will replace the Church as the teacher of ethics. No matter how hard some scientists might like to pretend that their ethical opinions are scientific, they're not. Our knowledge of what we *ought* to do will always have to come from outside science. In fact, to put it bluntly, it will always have to come from revelation.

Can the Church Survive Its Scandals?

Sometimes people point to recent scandals in the Church and say, "How can the Church possibly survive?" But the Church has been through a lot worse.

No one wants to trivialize the damage that abusive priests have done, both to their victims and to the priesthood itself. But when pop culture paints priests as especially prone to child abuse, pop culture is wrong. It turns out, when you look at the statistics, that Catholic priests are no more likely to be child abusers than are Protestant ministers or the general population.

That's still bad, because we feel instinctively that priests should be more virtuous than other people—even though we know they're sinners. But it does mean that, whenever you hear someone coming up with a supposedly scientific explanation of how celibacy drives priests to abuse children, you know that the explanation is wrong. It's making a fundamental scientific blunder: Before you attempt to explain a phenomenon, you must first make sure that the phenomenon exists.

If you explain why rocks fall up, and it turns out that they don't fall up, then your explanation is wrong. If you explain why priests are more likely to be abusive, and it turns out that priests aren't more likely to be abusive, then your explanation is wrong.

But it's also true that abuse cases are more likely to be reported in the Catholic Church—and ironically, that's because the Catholic Church is better at managing its clergy than are many other religions. In the archives of every diocese is a file for every one of its priests, and in each priest's file is every complaint—justified or not—that has ever been lodged against him. Nothing like that degree of record keeping goes on in most Protestant denominations, so it's impossible to see patterns of abuse if they exist.

The real abuse scandal was that, in some dioceses (certainly not all), the administration didn't act on the knowledge it had. There was no massive cover-up, whatever you may have seen on television. But there were some people who made really bad decisions, and we're all suffering from those decisions.

At any rate, however bad the scandals have been, the Church has survived worse. There were medieval popes who were political tools of the French kings. There were Renaissance popes who came from families of notorious poisoners. Yet the Church has always found the strength to purge itself, to reform what was wrong and hold fast to that which was good.

The Church that survived the Avignon era and the Medici and Borgia popes is not going to evaporate because of a few negative media stories. Long after the scandals are over, the Church will still be here for us. There will be new scandals, because there will always be sinners. But the Church knows how to deal with sin.

Into the Future

So what will the Catholic Church look like in the future?

A good look at the Church today will probably tell us. There are about 135 million Catholics in Africa, with the number growing rapidly. There are about the same number in Brazil alone, not counting the rest of South America. There are about 75 million in the Philippines. There are about 95 million in Mexico; there are about the same number in the United States.

As we've seen, the Church is growing by leaps and bounds exactly where the population of the world is growing by leaps and bounds. In Africa and Asia there are already millions of Catholics, and there will soon be millions more.

And we know that the Church is also growing in unexpected places. No one knows how many Catholics there are in China, for example, because the Chinese government refuses to allow the

Catholic Church as an institution. But reports are that the number is growing all the time.[1]

And in spite of the dire predictions, the Church isn't going away in Europe or in North America. There are still thousands of conversions every year, and millions of babies are born into Catholic families.

If you think that the Catholic Church's greatness is all in the past, try going to a World Youth Day. The spectacle of hundreds of thousands of young people eagerly jostling to catch even a glimpse of the Holy Father will quickly put to rest any notion that the Catholic Church is fading away. If these are the Catholics of the future, then the future must be bright indeed.

No matter where you look, the Catholic Church is there. And it's growing all the time. And it's still the same holy and apostolic Catholic Church. The Mass adapts to local traditions everywhere, but it's always the Mass. The sacraments may happen in a hundred different languages, but they're the same sacraments.

So we have a pretty good idea of what the Catholic Church will look like in the future: It will look like the human race—colorful, infinitely diverse, but all one family of God's children. It will be truly Catholic—a word that means "universal." It will be enriched by beautiful traditions from all over the planet.

Like the living body that it is, the Catholic Church will continue to grow and learn. But it will always be the same Catholic Church, always true to itself, and always faithful to the teachings of the apostles. Yours is this Church.

NOTES

CHAPTER ONE: *Yours Is the Church That Saved Civilization*

1. Adapted from Sidonius Apollinaris, *Letters*, O.M. Dalton, trans. (London: Oxford, 1915), bk. 2, chap. 9, p. 50, www.ccel.org.
2. Adapted from Gregory of Tours, *History of the Franks*, Ernest Brehaut, trans. (New York: Columbia University Press, 1916), preface, www.fordham.edu.
3. "The Prologue of Walafrid," in Eginhard, *Life of Charlemagne*, adapted from the translation in *Early Lives of Charlemagne*, A.J. Grant, ed. (London: A. Moring, De la More, 1905), pp. 1–2.

CHAPTER TWO: *Yours Is the Church That Nurtured Modern Science*

1. Gossuin of Metz, Gautier of Metz, Vincent of Beauvais, *Caxton's Mirrour of the World*, Oliver H. Prior, ed. (London: Early English Text Society, 1913), pp. 51–52. Modernized from Middle English.
2. Pope John Paul II, addressing participants in the Plenary Session of the Pontifical Academy of Sciences, October 31, 1992, no. 10, www.vatican.va.
3. See Anne Marie Riha, "Educating Our Children: Catholic Schools Doing More With Less," FoxNews.com, February 8, 2011; Liz Bowie, "Catholic Schools Do Well On Standardized Tests," *Baltimore Sun*, September 11, 2009, www.baltimoresun.com.

C

HAPTER

 T

HREE:

 Yours Is the Church of Charity

1. Gerhard Uhlhorn, *Christian Charity in the Ancient Church* (New York: Charles Scribner's Sons, 1883), p. 3.
2. Tertullian, *Apologetic* 2.39, adapted from the translation by William Reeves in *The Apologies of Justin Martyr, Tertullian, and Minutius Felix* (London: W. Churchill, 1716), pp. 308–309.
3. Clement of Alexandria, *Who Is the Rich Man That Shall Be Saved?* 3, adapted from the translation in Alexander Roberts and James Donaldson, eds., *The Writings of the Fathers Down to 325 AD: Vol. II: Fathers of the Second Century*, vol. 21, *The Ante-Nicene Fathers* (Buffalo, N.Y.: Christian Literature, 1885), p. 591.
4. Julian, quoted in Victor Duruy, *History of Rome and the Roman People* (Boston: Dana Estes and Charles E. Lauriat, 1887), volume VIII, p. 175.
5. Quoted in Duruy, pp. 175–176.
6. Julian, Epistle 49, adapted from the translation by John Duncombe in *Select Works of the Emperor Julian* (London: T. Cadell, 1784), vol. 2, pp. 127–130.
7. See Karl Hoeber, "Julian the Apostate," *The Catholic Encyclopedia*, vol. 8 (New York: Robert Appleton, 1910), www.newadvent.org.
8. Jerome, Letter 77, no. 6, adapted from the translation by W.H. Fremantle, *St. Jerome: Letters and Select Works*, vol. 6, *Nicene and Post-Nicene Fathers* (New York: Christian Literature, 1893), p. 160.
9. Jerome, Letter 77, no. 6.

CHAPTER FOUR: *Yours Is the Church That Made Music Great*

1. Gerhard Gietmann, "Ecclesiastical Music," *The Catholic Encyclopedia*, vol. 10 (New York: Robert Appleton, 1911), www.newadvent.org.
2. Gilbert Murray, *Euripides and His Age* (New York: Henry Holt, 1913), p. 14, www.newadvent.org.

CHAPTER FIVE: *Yours Is the Church That Inspired the Great Works of Art*

1. Decree of the Second Council of Nicea, AD 787, adapted from the translation in Henry R. Percival, *The Seven Ecumenical Councils*, Philip Schaff and Henry Wace, eds., vol. 14, *Nicene and Post-Nicene Fathers* (New York: Charles Scribner's Sons, 1900), p. 550.
2. Adapted from Giorgio Vasari, *Lives of the Painters, Sculptors and Architects*, A.B. Hinds, trans. (London: J.M. Dent, 1900), vol. 8.

CHAPTER SIX: *Yours Is the Church That Inspired Great Literature*

1. Jerome, Letter to St. Augustine, author's translation. See *The Confessions and Letters of St. Augustine, With a Sketch of His Life and Work*, Letter 195, vol. 1, *Nicene and Post-Nicene Fathers*, Philip Schaff, ed. (New York: Christian Literature, 1886), p. 556.
2. St. Augustine, *Confessions*, bk. 1, chap. 7, no. 1, adapted from the translation by Richard Challoner (Dublin: Farrell Kiernan, 1770), pp. 13–14.
3. Dante, *Inferno*, canto 1, 1–6, author's translation.
4. G.K. Chesterton, *Orthodoxy* (Chicago: Moody Bible Institute, 2009), p. 137.

CHAPTER SEVEN: *Yours Is the Church That Made Women People*
1. Homer, *Iliad,* book 3, George Chapman, trans. (London: Chatto and Windus, 1885), p. 162.

CHAPTER EIGHT: *Yours Is the Church That Made Children People*
1. See Celsus, *De medicina,* W.G. Spence, trans. (London: Heinemann, 1938).
2. Tertullian, *De Anima* 25, adapted from Peter Holmes, trans., *The Writings of Tertullian, Vol. 2,* vol. 15, *Ante-Nicene Christian Library* (London: T. & T. Clark, 1870), p. 470.
3. Plutarch, "Life of Lycurgus," adapted from *Plutarch's Lives, The Translation Called Dryden's, Corrected from the Greek and Revised by A. H. Clough* (New York: Little, Brown, 1906), pp. 86–87.

CHAPTER NINE: *Yours Is the Church of Human Dignity*
1. "Negro," *Encyclopedia Britannica,* Eleventh Edition, vol. 19, p. 344.
2. See Francis Augustus Macnutt, *Bartholomew de las Casas: His Life, His Apostolate, and His Writings* (Whitefish, Mont.: Kessinger, 2010), p. 69.
3. Quoted in Ambrus Miskolczy, *Hitler's Library* (Budapest: Central European University Press, 2003), p. 25.

CHAPTER TEN: *Yours Is the Church of World Peace*
1. Adapted from a quote in Bradley Lightbody, *The Second World War: Ambitions to Nemesis* (London: Routledge, 2004), p. 39.

CHAPTER ELEVEN: *Yours Is the Church of the Future*
1. See Philip Jenkins, "Who's counting China? Phenomenal growth in the number of Christians," available at www.christiancentury.org.

About the Author

Mike Aquilina is the author or editor of more than thirty books on Catholic history, doctrine, and devotion. He has cohosted eight series for EWTN and is a frequent guest on Catholic radio. His publishing career spans almost three decades, and hundreds of his articles have appeared in periodicals in the United States and abroad.